Leidenschaft Vorarlberg
Fotografien von Peter Mathis, Texte von Alfons J. Kopf

A Passion for Vorarlberg
Photographs by Peter Mathis, Texts by Alfons J. Kopf

W0316773

IMPRESSUM

Editors and Publishers: Peter Mathis and Jürgen Höfle

Peter Mathis Photographs KEG
Erlachstrasse 45, 6845 Hohenems, Austria
ww.mathis-photographs.com

Höfle Offsetdruckerei GmbH
Marktstrasse 61, 6850 Dornbirn, Austria
www.hoefle.at

Photos: ©Peter Mathis
Text: ©Alfons J. Kopf
Graphics: Karsten Kubitz, Höfle Offsetdruckerei GmbH
Pre-Press: Gudrun Fenkart
Printed: Höfle Offsetdruckerei GmbH

This book was written and illustrated with all due care and attention. No responsibility, however, is taken for the correctness of the information. It is hence not possible for either the author or the publishing house to assume responsibility for any damages or disadvantages that may result from the references contained within the work.

ISBN 978-3-200-01289-9
©2008 Peter Mathis, Jürgen Höfle, 1. Circulation
All rights reserved. Reprinting in whole or in part, as well as distribution via film, radio and television, and photographic reproduction in any format, is only possible with the written authorization of the publisher.

Image, front cover:
A Passion for Vorarlberg - not an uncontrollable intoxication, but a quiet, stirring enthusiasm. The two forest farmhouses of the Berchtold family in the area of Oberkaltberg in the Schwarzenberg commune are a fitting representation. The view stretches into the rear of the Bregenz Forest.

Image, right page:
Hikers on the Kanisfluh mountain range in the Bregenz Forest heading towards the peak of mount Holenke (2,044 m).

Herausgeber und Verleger: Peter Mathis und Jürgen Höfle

Peter Mathis Photographs KEG
Erlachstraße 45, 6845 Hohenems, Austria
www.mathis-photographs.com

Höfle Offsetdruckerei GmbH
Marktstraße 61, 6850 Dornbirn, Austria
www.hoefle.at

Fotos: ©Peter Mathis
Text: ©Alfons J. Kopf
Layout und Gestaltung: Karsten Kubitz, Höfle Offsetdruckerei GmbH
Druckvorstufe: Gudrun Fenkart
Druck: Höfle Offsetdruckerei GmbH

Dieses Buch wurde mit aller Sorgfalt geschrieben und bebildert. Dennoch müssen alle Angaben ohne Gewähr erfolgen. Weder dem Autor noch dem Verlag und Herausgeber ist es deshalb möglich, für Nachteile oder Schäden, die aus den gemachten praktischen Hinweisen resultieren, eine Haftung zu übernehmen.

ISBN 978-3-200-01289-9
©2008 Peter Mathis, Jürgen Höfle, 1. Auflage
Alle Rechte vorbehalten. Nachdruck, auch auszugsweise, sowie Verbreitung durch Film, Funk und Fernsehen, durch fotomechanische Wiedergabe, Tonträger und DV-Verarbeitungssysteme jeder Art nur mit schriftlicher Genehmigung der Herausgeber.

Bild Umschlag vorne:
Leidenschaft Vorarlberg – kein unkontrollierter Rausch, eher eine stille Begeisterung, die in sich ruht. Die beiden Wälder Bauernhäuser der Familie Berchtold in der Parzelle Oberkaltberg, Gemeinde Schwarzenberg, sind eine passende Darstellung. Der Blick geht in den Hinteren Bregenzerwald.

Bild rechte Seite:
Wanderer auf dem Bergmassiv der Kanisfluh im Bregenzerwald auf dem Weg zum Hauptgipfel Holenke (2.044 m)

Peter Mathis | Alfons J. Kopf

LEIDENSCHAFTVORARLBERG

Vorarlberg von seiner schönsten Seite. Das 900-Seelen-Dorf Schoppernau liegt im sogenannten „Hinterwald", also dem hinteren Teil des Bregenzerwaldes. Die Talschaft mit ihren 22 selbstständigen Gemeinden ist altes Bauernland und in mancher Hinsicht typisch für die Besiedelungssituation in Vorarlberg. Das 1710 erbaute Barockkirchlein „Zu den hl. Aposteln Philipp und Jakob" hebt sich hier ab von der imposanten Südflanke der Kanisfluh.

Vorarlberg from its most attractive side: the village of Schoppernau, home to a mere 900 souls, is situated in the so-called 'Hinterwald', the part of the Bregenz forest which is located to the rear of Bregenz. With its 22 independent communes, this district is old farming country and in most respects typical of the settlement situation in Vorarlberg. The baroque church 'To the Holy Apostles of Philip and Jacob' stands silhouetted against the imposing southern flank of mount Kanisfluh.

„Alt Ems" über der Stadt Hohenems war dereinst eine der größten Burganlagen weitum, 800 m lang und bis zu 85 m breit. Im Appenzellerkrieg 1407 zerstört, wurde sie von den Emser Grafen wieder aufgebaut. Erst als Hohenems anno 1765 österreichisch wurde, schlug die – beinah – letzte Stunde der Burg: Sie wurde 1792 auf Abbruch versteigert. Die Reste der Ruinen zumindest sollen wieder fachgerecht erhalten werden.

Alt Ems, above the town of Hohenems, was once one of the region's biggest castle structures, 800 m long and up to 85 m wide. Destroyed in 1407 during the Appenzell war, it was rebuilt by the Ems counts. The castle survived until 1765, when the Hohenems region became part of Austria. It then declined before being auctioned off for demolition in 1792. The remnants of the ruins are under order of preservation.

Das Werden einer Kulturlandschaft Becoming a Cultural Landscape

BESIEDELUNG SETTLEMENT

Lautes Lachen klingt von der Subersach hinauf zur Gschwendtobelbrücke, der alten Verbindung zwischen Großdorf und Lingenau im Bregenzerwald. Etliche Meter unterhalb der gedeckten Holzbrücke liefern einander einige Männer einen fröhlichen Bewerb. Die Hosenbeine hochgekrempelt, wetteifern sie darum, einen flachen Stein so zu werfen, dass er möglichst oft auf dem klaren Wasser des Baches hüpft. Wir beobachten keinen Schulausflug, da haben Spitzenmanager aus Großkonzernen ihren Spaß, gemeinsam mit Mediengrößen. Sie überbrücken die kurze Wartezeit, bis ihnen für die Geburtstagsfeier eines Freundes eine Vorarlberger Spezialität serviert wird: Kässpätzle, frisch zubereitet in einem besonderen Lokal.

Knapp über der fröhlichen Truppe werkt inzwischen auf der Brücke die Köchin und reibt den Spätzleteig in kochendes Wasser. Drei verschiedene heimische Käsesorten werden unter die fertigen Spätzle gemischt, obenauf runden schließlich gedünstete Zwiebelringe die Leibspeise vieler Vorarlberger ab. Die fröhlichen Manager lassen sich gern verwöhnen nach ihrer Expedition ins Tobel, es sitzt sich gemütlich auf der Brücke, die 1835 nach Plänen des Alois Negrelli erbaut wurde. Von dem Herrn stammen auch wesentliche Pläne für den Suezkanal, ebenso für die Regulierung des Alpenrheins und etliche Bauwerke in Vorarlberg. Seine Brücke im Bregenzerwald konnte stehen bleiben, als sich der Verkehr einen anderen Weg suchte, und so nützen sie neben Radfahrern und Wanderern eben auch Feinschmecker.

Solche Erlebnisse sind es unter anderem, die Vorarlberg zur Leidenschaft werden lassen. Denn es mag zwar ungerecht sein, aber es kann nicht jeder den Vorzug genießen, das Licht der Welt in Vorarlberg zu erblicken und hier aufwachsen zu dürfen. Deshalb zieht es Gäste ebenso ins Land zwischen Bodensee und Arlberg wie neue Einwohner. Die Bevölkerungszahl hat deutlich zugenommen. Um die Jahrhundertwende 1900 zählte das Land 129.240 Einwohner, heute (2008) sind es 367.000.

Es ist ja nicht getan mit einer kunstvollen Holzbrücke über die Subersach und mit Kässpätzle. Vorarlberg hat einiges mehr zu bieten an Landschaft, an Kultur, an Überraschungen. Dabei glänzt Österreichs westlichstes Bundesland gewiss nicht etwa durch Größe oder Sensationen. Nach dem höchsten aller Berge oder der tiefsten Schlucht sucht man vergebens. Was beeindruckt ist wohl die einzigartige Kombination von Riedwiesen und sanften Hügeln, von Tälern und auch von schroffen Felsen, die hier auf kleinem Raum miteinander harmonieren. Vorarlberg ist ein Land der kurzen Wege, es ist gefühlte Nähe. Zudem ist das Land wirtschaftlich stark. Was die Industrie produziert, geht zu 80 Prozent in den Export, in manchen Branchen sind es an die 100 Prozent.

Wer macht aber gern Urlaub im Industriegebiet? Nun, es ist keine Großindustrie zu finden in Vorarlberg und die meisten Betriebe konzentrieren sich auf das bevölkerungsreiche Rheintal und den Walgau. Darf ich kurz meine eigene Situation schildern: Überfällt mich der Drang, mich sportlich zu geben, so laufe ich an sechs oder sieben Gewerbebetrieben vorbei. Danach bin ich bereits in der Grünzone und wechsle nach wenigen hundert Metern sogar ins Naturschutzgebiet – im Rheindelta befindet sich das größte Feuchtgebiet am Bodenseeufer.

Hier kommen Tourismus, Landwirtschaft und Natur miteinander klar. Das ging einst nicht ohne Auseinandersetzungen ab, inzwischen aber sind Fasane und Reiher, Rehe und Frösche wohlgelitten. Jogger und Walker, Radler und Spaziergänger staunen da ob dem Sprung der Rehe, die davoneilen zum nächstliegenden Gebüsch oder Wäldchen.

Gerade erst haben sich die Berufsfischer vom Bodensee über die Wasserqualität beklagt. Nein, eben nicht zu schmutzig sei das Wasser im See, sondern viel zu sauber. Das bremst das Wachstum von Algen und anderem Futter der Fische. Hecht, Felchen und Zander wachsen deshalb nicht mehr so rasch wie früher, als der Phosphateintrag aus den Waschmaschinen der reinlichen Bevölkerung noch für erheblich mehr Dünger und damit auch für reichere Beute sorgte.

Mit dem See sind wir wieder beim Wasser und bei der Subersach. „Subr", das meint auf alemannisch „sauber" und ist ein Hinweis auf die Sprachkultur im Land. Angelehnt an das Mittelhochdeutsche haben die Alemannen einst eine Lautverschiebung

Loud laughter can be heard from the Subersach river to the Gschwendtobelbrücke bridge, the age-old connection between Großdorf and Lingenau in the Bregenz Forest region. Some metres below the covered wooden bridge, a group of men are taking part in a friendly competition. Their trousers turned up, they compete with each other by throwing flat stones into the stream such that they bounce off the clear water as many times as possible. We aren't watching a school outing, but top managers from large companies enjoying themselves together with some media celebrities. They're making up the time until they're due to be served a speciality from the Vorarlberg region for a friend's birthday celebration: so-called cheese spätzle, freshly made in a special restaurant. Just above the cheerful group of men, the chef is hard at work on the bridge, rubbing the spätzle dough in boiling water. When it is ready, three different kinds of cheese from the region are then mixed with the spätzle, before the fried onion rings on top complete what is the favourite dish of many people in Vorarlberg. The cheerful managers are only too ready to be spoilt after their expedition to the Tobel [ravine], and the bridge is a cosy place, having been built in 1835 according to the plans of Alois Negrelli. Negrelli also contributed key architectural plans to the Suez Canal as well as to the regulation of the Alpenrhein and to numerous buildings in Vorarlberg.
His bridge in the Bregenz Forest was allowed to remain standing after local traffic was routed away from it, which is why the bridge is now used by cyclists and hikers as well as gourmets. Such experiences are one of the reasons why the Vorarlberg region has become a passion for so many visitors. It may seem unfair, but not everyone can be lucky enough to be born and grow up in Vorarlberg - of all the beautiful places in the world. It is this beauty that has attracted visitors and new inhabitants alike to the region between Lake Constance and the Arlberg, and why its population has increased significantly. Around the turn of the century 1900, the region had 129,240 inhabitants, today (2008) 367,000 live in Vorarlberg.

Yet with regard to landscapes, culture and surprises, Vorarlberg has more to offer than just an artistic wooden bridge over the Subersach and its cheese spätzle. It is also neither the size nor her distractions that make Austria's most western region stand out. Neither the highest of Austria's mountains nor the deepest of her ravines can be found here. It is rather the unique combination of reed meadows and gentle hills, of valleys and of jagged rocks which blend together here in such a small space which is so impressive. Vorarlberg is a region with short paths and with a tangible feeling of closeness. And it is also a strong economic region: 80 percent of what is produced in its different industries is for export; in certain industries it is nearly 100 percent.

But who wants to spend their holidays in an industrial region? Well, Vorarlberg isn't a region of heavy industry, and most of the companies are based in the densely populated Rhine valley and Walgau. Please allow me to provide a brief description of my own situation here: if I feel the urge to be sporty, I jog past six or seven enterprises. Then, I'm already in the countryside and after another hundred metres or so, the nature protection area starts – the Rhine delta, the largest wetland area, which is situated along the shores of Lake Constance.

But tourism, agriculture and nature all co-exist successfully here, too. This co-existence, however, may not have been achieved without disputes, but now pheasants and herons, deer and frogs are well-established. Joggers and walkers, cyclists and strollers marvel at the jumping deer hurrying off to the nearest shrubbery or small woods.

In recent times, the professional fishermen of Lake Constance have complained about the water quality: the water in the lake isn't too dirty for them, but rather too clean. Clean water hampers the growth of algae and other feed for the fish. This has meant that Luce, whitefish and pike no longer grow as quickly as they used to when the phosphate discharge from the washing machines of the population around the lake supplied significantly more fertiliser and the subsequent algae growth guaranteed abundant prey.

Es reift allerhand im Land, keineswegs nur bei den Gartenbaubetrieben und Bauern. In der Umgebung größerer Gemeinden pflegen Pächter liebevoll ihre Schrebergärten, wo Gemüse für den Eigenbedarf geerntet werden kann. An den langen Stiegeln, den Bohnenstangen also, sollen Bohnen emporranken.

All kinds of products are grown in the Vorarlberg region, and not just at the market gardens and farms. Around the bigger communes, leaseholders lovingly maintain allotments where vegetables are often grown for their own kitchens. The longer poles - bean poles - assist the runner beans in their climb upwards.

versäumt und vergessen deshalb auch beim „Hus" das „a". Die Subersach führt demnach also besonders sauberes Wasser. Und Einheimische, die während einer Bergwanderung ihren Durst am plätschernden Bach stillen, sind die erstaunten Blicke von Gästen gewöhnt. Ja, ist das denn nicht gefährlich, so ganz ohne Abkochen, völlig ohne Schutz?
Nein, ist es nicht. Und „subr" ist in Vorarlberg keineswegs nur das Wasser. Eine hübsche junge Frau ist da eben „a subrs Moatle" und ein ehrliches, gutes Geschäft „a subre Sach". Verständlich, dass die Vorarlberger ihre Heimat ebenfalls als „subrs Ländle" besingen. Dazu trägt gewiss die akkurate Pflege dieser Landschaft durch die Bauern bei. Bis hoch hinauf unter die Gipfel von Silvretta, Verwall und Rätikon trotzt ein traditionsbewusster Bauernstand auch den steilsten Berghängen noch Ertrag ab. Immerhin 23 % der Landesfläche von gerade einmal 2.601 km^2 sind Alpen (in anderen deutschsprachigen Gebieten als Almen bekannt), Viehweiden, die nur während bestimmter Sommermonate bestoßen sind, auf die also über den Sommer Vieh aufgetrieben wird.

Anno 1880, als mit dem Bau des Bahntunnels durch den Arlberg begonnen wurde, der Vorarlberg mit dem Rest Österreichs verband, betrug der Anteil landwirtschaftlicher Bevölkerung noch rund 55 %, heute sind es gerade noch 2 %. Die meisten Bauern üben einen zweiten Beruf aus, viele der 4.000 bäuerlichen Betriebe funktionieren, weil die ganze Familie mit anpackt.

Zudem sind ein Gutteil der Vorarlberger Bauern nach wie vor Teilzeitnomaden. Die meiste Zeit im Jahr leben sie in ihren Höfen im Tal und in Talnähe. Ende Mai, Anfang Juni wird auf das Vorsäß oder Maisäß auf etwa 1.000 Höhenmeter übersiedelt, im Sommer geht es noch einmal 1.000 m weiter bergwärts auf eine der 560 Hochalpen. Im Herbst schließlich erfolgt, angepasst an die Wettersituation, der Rückweg ebenfalls in zwei Etappen. Diese traditionelle Form der Dreistufenwirtschaft trägt wesentlich dazu bei, dass die Hügel und Berge im Land gepflegt sind und nicht verbuschen.

Talking about the lake brings us back to water and the Subersach. "Subr" means "clean" in Alemannic and refers to the linguistic culture of the region. Similar to Middle High German, the Alemannic dialect missed out on a sound shift and therefore, for instance, does not insert an "a" in the word "Hus" [Haus, house]. This means that the waters of the Subersach must be clean - and that locals frequently marvel at the surprised looks on the faces of visitors, who often watch their local guides quenching their thirst in this lively stream during mountain hikes high up in the Montafon. „But isn't it dangerous to drink that water without boiling it or purifying it?" No, it isn't. And the water isn't the only thing in Vorarlberg that is „subr". A beautiful young woman is called „a subrs Moatle" and a fair, good deal is "a subre Sach". It is therefore understandable that the people in Vorarlberg sing about their homeland as being a "subrs Ländle" [a clean country]. The local farmers also contribute to this title by appropriately cultivating the land. The traditional farmers harvest their crops from even the steepest slopes and up to the highest peaks of Silvretta, Verwall and Rätikon. After all, just 23 % of an area which totals only 2,601 km² are meadows (in the German-speaking regions known as Alpen or Almen) – alpine pastures that are only used during certain summer months and where the cattle also ascends to graze.

In 1880, when the construction of the railway tunnel through the Arlberg to connect Vorarlberg with the rest of Austria started, the share of the population working in agriculture was about 55 %; today this share has fallen to a mere 2 %. Today, most farmers have a second job and many of the 4,000 farms are only able to exist because the whole family helps in the business.

Moreover, most of the farmers in Vorarlberg live as temporary nomads. Most of the time, they live on their farms in the valley and near the valley. By the end of May or the beginning of June, they relocate to the so-called Vorsäß or Maisäß [advanced pastures] at a height of approximately 1,000 metres. In the summer, their cattle are then taken up another 1,000 metres to graze on one of the 561 alpine pastures. In the autumn, depending on the weather situation, the descent back to the valley is divided into two stages as well. This traditional form of seasonal migration contributes significantly to the fact that the hills and mountains in this region are cultivated and not overgrown.

Alpine farming is also one of the reasons for the outstanding quality of the local milk, butter, cheese and meat. In the mountains, the 39,000 cattle do not get additional feed, and additive-free food is produced in the 137 alpine dairies. But of course, neither the conservation of the landscape nor the quality of the feed represents the reasons for this quite laborious way of farming. Quite simply, the feed supply in the valley is not sufficient to care for the cattle all year round. And while the cattle are on the alpine pastures, the hay for the winter months can be made in the valley.

The innkeepers and the chefs in the region also benefit from the naturally produced food of the farmers and other local suppliers in Vorarlberg. Don't use the word 'provincial' here: no other region in Austria has so many star-rated restaurants as Vorarlberg. The region has 47 gourmet restaurants, which is almost exactly 10 % of the total number of stars in Austria. And don't forget that Vorarlberg only accounts for 4.3 % of the total population of Austria.

And it goes without saying that the locals as well as their visitors appreciate living in a region with such culinary delights.

In addition to the star-rated restaurants in the restaurant guides, there are also the 'insider tip' restaurants – which, to the disappointment of the insiders, are no longer a secret. Those who dismiss the restaurants they pass by on their travels, because they cannot imagine that such places can really offer anything of worth only have themselves to blame. Many restaurants in the valleys and the towns can offer cultivated and sophisticated hospitality.

In this sense, we have Wolfgang of the "Anker" in Fußach with his "Bodensee-Variationen", composed of baked perch, whitefish filet, catfish and pike in a sauce made from white wine. This menu, however, is only served between November and April, since the preparation of such menus is too time-consuming during the opening time of the garden restaurant in the summer. And along with the closeness to the habitat of the fish, time is of the essence with such a freshly made fish quartet.

Die Wasserqualität im Bodensee bereitet den Berufsfischern derzeit Sorgen. Nicht etwa wegen Verschmutzung, denn das Wasser ist zu sauber und deshalb wachsen die Fische nicht mehr so rasch wie vor 15, 20 Jahren! Was den 16 Berufsfischern am Vorarlberger Seeufer geringere Erträge beschert, stört die Angler kaum: Für sie ist das Fischen vom Ufer aus Erholung pur. Wenn keiner beißt – was soll's. Und ist der Fisch nicht groß genug – zurück ins Wasser damit. An die 8.000 Hobbyfischer sind registriert. Rechts: Schilfbestand vor dem Seeufer am Rohrspitz in Fußach.

Die Alpwirtschaft ist aber auch eine der Grundlagen für herausragende Qualität an Milch, Butter und Käse sowie an Fleisch. Oben am Berg wird den 39.000 Rindviechern gar nichts zugefüttert, in den 137 Alpsennereien entstehen unverfälschte Lebensmittel. Natürlich waren aber weder Landschaftspflege noch Futterqualität der Grund für diese doch aufwändige Art der Bewirtschaftung. Es ist schlicht das Futterangebot in Tallagen nicht ausreichend, um das Vieh das Jahr über zu versorgen. Und während die Rinder auf den Alpen sind, wird im Tal das Heu für die Wintermonate eingebracht.

Von den naturnah produzierten Lebensmitteln der Vorarlberger Bauern und anderer heimischer Lieferanten profitieren auch die Gastwirte, die Köchinnen und Köche im Land. Von wegen Provinz: Nirgends in Österreich finden sich so viele Haubenlokale wie im Ländle Vorarlberg. 47 sind es, also ziemlich genau 10 % der Hauben-Gesamtzahl in Österreich. Dabei hat Vorarlberg gerade einmal einen Anteil von 4,3 % der Bevölkerung Österreichs.
Die Vorarlbergerinnen und Vorarlberger wissen es selbstverständlich ebenso zu schätzen wie die Gäste, dass sie in einer Genussregion leben. Zusätzlich zu den Spitzenlokalen aus den Restaurantführern gibt es die Geheimtipps, die meisten davon sind allerdings zum Leidwesen der Insider längst nicht mehr geheim. Wer an manchen Lokalen im Land vorbeifährt, weil er sich nicht vorstellen kann, dass es in einem solchen Haus viel Gutes zu probieren gibt, der ist selber schuld. Zahlreiche Häuser in den Talschaften und Städten setzen auf gepflegte Gastlichkeit.
Da ist etwa Wolfgang vom „Anker" in Fußach mit seinen „Bodensee-Variationen", komponiert aus Egli gebacken, Felchenfilet, Wels sowie Zander in Weißweinsauce. Serviert wird solches allerdings nur zwischen November und April, weil während der Gastgartenzeit die für solch aufwändige Menüs erforderliche Zeit fehlt. Und bei einem frisch zubereiteten Fischquartett ist Zeit ein entscheidender Faktor, wie auch die Nähe zum Lebensraum dieser Fische.

Besiedelt seit der Steinzeit

Am Bodensee, im ganzen Rheintal und in anderen Landesteilen sind markante Spuren uralter Besiedelung und Wanderbewegungen zu finden, die weit vor Christi Geburt zurückreichen. Ein besonders eindrucksvoller Fund gelang am Bärenkopf im Kleinwalsertal. Dort schlugen vor rund 8.000 Jahren Handwerker Werkzeug aus Stein aus dem Felsen, ein uraltes Bergwerk also. Im Montafon zeugen Siedlungen aus der Bronzezeit von durchgehender Nutzung als Lebensraum.
Ab dem 4. und 5. Jahrhundert v.Chr. schließlich waren anscheinend die Kelten hier zugange, ab 15 v.Chr. beherrschten die Römer mit Rätien auch das heutige Vorarlberg. Der römische Kaiser Tiberius, so wird berichtet, obsiegte im ersten auf dem Bodensee bezeugten Seegefecht gegen heimische Seefahrer.

Wir Alemannen...

Germanentruppen und schließlich die besondere Gruppe der Alemannen traten gegen die römische Westgrenze an und setzen sich im 5. oder 6. Jahrhundert nach Christi Geburt im Bodenseegebiet fest. In den südlichen Talschaften des Landes hingegen, wo Vorarlberg an den Teil der Schweiz grenzt, wo heute noch rätoromanisch gesprochen wird, hielten sich die Rätoromanen. Sie hinterließen uns Namen und Ortsbezeichnungen, die bis heute gelten.

Seither zogen immer wieder kleine und größere Gruppen an Zuwanderern in das Land vor dem Arlberg – die Legende von den angeblich rein „alemannischen" Vorarlbergern hält sich trotzdem zäh. Dazu passt, dass weder Herkunft noch Bezeichnung der Alemannen irgendwie gesichert sind: Raue Germanenstämme halt, von römischen Autoren unter der Bezeichnung „Alamannen" zusammengefasst. Und was heute als alemannischer Dialekt angesehen wird, muss mit diesen Scharen aber schon auch gar nichts zu tun gehabt haben. Wie auch immer, das Alemannische klingt anders und ist anders.

The quality of the water is currently a source of anxiety to professional fishermen. And it isn't because of pollution, but because the water is actually too clean, which means that the fish aren't growing as quickly as they used to 15 or 20 years ago. But the problems of the 16 professional fishermen on the banks of this lake in Vorarlberg aren't of concern to the anglers. For them, fishing from the banks is a favourite way to relax. They don't really mind if they don't get a bite. And if a fish isn't big enough, it's simply thrown back in. 8,000 hobby anglers are registered in this region. Right: reeds in front of the banks of the lake at Rohrspitz in Fußach.

Populated since the Stone Age

At Lake Constance, in the entire Rhine valley and other regions, distinctive traces of ancient settlements and nomadic movements can be found which date back to long before the birth of Christ. At the Bärenkopf in the Little Walser Valley, a particular impressive discovery has been made. About 8,000 years ago, craftsmen cut tools from the rocks - an ancient mine so to speak. In the Montafon, settlements from the Bronze Age are evidence of this area's long use as an area of settlement.

From the 4th and 5th century B.C. onwards, Celts populated the area; from 15 B.C., the Romans with Rätien controlled what is the current Vorarlberg region. The Roman emperor Tiberius, as locals will tell you, won against the local seamen in the first attested naval fight on Lake Constance.

We, the Alemanni ...

German troops, and later the particular group of the Alemanni, did battle at the Roman western border and established themselves permanently in the Lake Constance region in the 5th or 6th century after the birth of Christ. In the southern valleys of the country, however, where Vorarlberg still borders the Rhaeto-Romanic-speaking part of Switzerland to this day, the Rhaeto-Romans lingered on and left us names and place names that are still used today.

Since then, smaller and larger groups of immigrants have been attracted by the land before the Arlberg – the legend of the supposedly pure "Alemannic" Vorarlberg inhabitants, however, persists. This is in line with the fact that neither the origin nor the name of the Alemanni is backed up by hard proof: they were just random Germanic clans summed up by the Roman authors under the name "alamanni". And what is currently regarded as the Alemannic dialect may have nothing to do with those ancient tribes. Whatever the truth, Alemannic sounds different and is different.

Settlement not only refers to the people who settle in a particular country, it also means the houses that are built by the people when they settle in the area. Over many centuries, with the exception of some stately manors, people have largely built farmyards and small cottages that are spread over the whole region in street villages and scattered villages. Many examples of the farmers' way of life still impress today and are surprisingly diverse for such a small region. The old farmyards in the Rhine valley, the Walser Valley and the Montafon can be distinguished between very easily.

Türme unterschiedlicher Art ragen in Vorarlberg empor.
Links St. Wolfgang, das neugotische Kirchlein der kleinen Bergparzelle Meschach ob Götzis.
Die Mittelweiherburg in Hard am Bodensee (erbaut 1560-1570) birgt seit einigen Jahren ein Textildruckmuseum. Hier eröffnete 1794 Samuel Vogel eine Cottondruckerei, die 1879/80 zum ersten dokumentierten Umweltstreit in Vorarlberg führte: Die Unterlieger am Dorfbach beschwerten sich heftig darüber, dass gefärbte Stoffballen im Bach ausgewaschen wurden. Der erzürnte Textilunternehmer schloss daraufhin kurzerhand die Fabrik, 200 Beschäftigte verloren ihre Arbeit. Ganz rechts der alte Fabrikturm (1884) des Gewerbeparks in Rankweil mit der Basilika, der Liebfrauenkirche von Rankweil, einem beliebten Wallfahrtsziel.

Besiedelung, das meint aber nie nur die Menschen, die sesshaft sind in einem bestimmten Land, das meint auch die Behausungen, die sie sich bauen, wenn Land besiedelt wird. Das waren in Vorarlberg lange Jahrhunderte hindurch, bis auf wenige Ausnahmen herrschaftlicher Bauten, nur Bauernhöfe und Katen, in Straßen- und Streusiedlungen aufgeteilt auf das ganze Land. Viele der Beispiele bäuerlicher Wohnkultur vermögen noch heute zu beeindrucken und zeigen erstaunliche Vielfalt für ein so kleines Land. Diese alten Bauernhöfe im Rheintal, im Bregenzerwald, im Walsertal oder im Montafon sind gut zu unterscheiden.

Markante Ausnahmen inmitten des Bauernlandes sind mittelalterliche Städtchen wie Feldkirch und Bludenz oder die Oberstadt von Bregenz. Beeindruckend die jüdische Geschichte der Stadt Hohenems, wo Christenviertel und Judenviertel relativ gut erhalten sind. Besonders das jüdische Erbe wird inzwischen wieder geschätzt, manche Ignoranz und Sünde der Vergangenheit, besonders an der Bausubstanz, mit viel Einfühlungsvermögen gut gemacht.

In den Jahrzehnten nach dem Ende des 2. Weltkrieges aber setzte sich durch, was als „Hüslebauer-Mentalität" der Vorarlberger weit über die Landesgrenzen bekannt ist: Das eigene Haus im eigenen Garten wurde zum erklärten Lebensziel vieler Vorarlberger und zahllose Wohnhäuser entstanden nach dem Grundplan „vier Wände und ein Satteldach".

Vor gut 20 Jahren aber hielt endlich wieder Qualität Einzug in die Planung der eigenen vier Wände. Ob Einfamilienhaus oder Wohnanlage – die junge Garde Vorarlberger Planer besann sich auf bewährte Traditionen. In Kombination mit aktuellen Erkenntnissen entstand eine bestaunenswerte Vorarlberger Bauschule mit mannigfaltigen Beispielen für durchdachtes Bauen und Wohnen. Verständlich, dass diese Entwicklung inzwischen von fachkundigen Besuchern in organisierten Reisen besichtigt wird.
Vorarlberg ist gewiss kein Reservat mit Eingeborenen, deren einzige Aufgabe es ist, für Gäste zu posieren. Das Land ist Lebensraum und Wirtschaftsstandort, ebenso aber beliebtes Ziel für Urlauber und Ausflügler. Es lässt sich hier stundenlang wandern, ohne mit der Zivilisation in Berührung zu kommen. Auch Skitouren erschließen beeindruckende Gebiete ohne jede menschliche Behausung. Aber für Einsiedler ist das Land nicht gedacht, sondern für Menschen, die Ruhe ebenso genießen können wie den Vorteil, richtig verwöhnt zu werden. Und wer die Kombination sucht aus beidem, der landet in Vorarlberg einen Volltreffer.

Dass es dennoch Menschen gibt, die hier aufwachsen und dann anderswo ihr Glück versuchen, gehört mit zu den Geschichten, die man sich erzählt. Da gibt es den Auswanderer, der im fernen Südafrika auf einen deutschen Arbeitskollegen trifft und diesem schließlich erzählt, dass er nahe von Bregenz am Bodensee aufgewachsen sei. Der Kollege kann das nicht begreifen. „Da war ich doch auch schon, das kenne ich! Wie kann man nur vom schönsten Platz der Erde wegziehen!"

Unvergessen auch die Anekdote aus einem Wirtshaus in Vorarlberg. Da lauscht ein Urlauber längere Zeit den Erzählungen eines Einheimischen über Amerika. Schließlich wagt er zu fragen, wie lange der Erzähler denn in den USA gelebt habe. „Ich, weshalb ich? Mein Bruder, der – hat immer auswandern wollen . . ."
Na ja, es gibt ja Fotobände, damit von Heimweh geplagte Vorarlberger ein Stück Heimat mit sich tragen können.

Many different kinds of tower project upwards in Vorarlberg.
Left: St. Wolfgang, the neo gothic chapel of the mountain parish of Meschach above Götzis.
Castle Mittelweiherburg in Hard am Bodensee, built from 1560-1570, has been home to a textiles museum for some years. It was here that Samuel Vogel opened a cotton printing workshop which in 1879/80 led to the first documented environmental dispute in Vorarlberg: those dwelling downstream in the village complained heavily about the coloured cotton which kept on being washed down the river. The angry owner of the textiles business was forced to close his factory, with 200 workers losing their jobs.
Far right: the old factory tower (1884) of Rankweil industrial estate with the basilica, the Church of Our Lady, Rankweil, a popular place of pilgrimage.

Some striking exceptions in this farming region are small medieval towns like Feldkirch and Bludenz or the upper town of Bregenz. The Jewish history of the town Hohenems is also impressive, where the Christian and the Jewish quarters are relatively well preserved. The Jewish heritage in particular is now appreciated once more; some of the ignorance and sins of the past - in particular as regards buildings - are being redressed with great sensitivity.

In the centuries after the end of the Second World War, however, the "Hüslebauer-Mentalität" [my home is my castle mentality] of the inhabitants of Vorarlberg, also known beyond the borders of the region, started to catch on: a house with a garden was the declared goal of many people living in the region and numerous houses were built according to the basic design of „four walls and a gable roof".

Finally, some 20 years ago, quality became the priority in the planning of houses once more. Whether in detached houses or housing estates, the young school of designers from Vorarlberg made use of proven traditions, which in combination with current findings have created an amazing regional school of construction with numerous examples of sophisticated constructions and decors. It is understandable that such architecture now attracts professional visitors in organised tours.

Vorarlberg cannot be described as a touristy place with native people whose only task is to pose for the visitors. The region is a home and a business location alike and a popular destination for holidaymakers and excursionists at the same time. Visitors can hike for hours without encountering civilisation; skiing tours lead through impressive regions without any human settlements. Yet the region isn't intended for recluses, but for people who cherish quietness just as much as they enjoy being pampered for a while. And those who aspire towards a combination of both of these things are likely to feel at home in Vorarlberg.

The fact that there are, of course people who grow up in this region and try their luck living somewhere else, also belongs to the stories that are told in the region. One such story is of an emigrant meeting a German colleague in faraway South-Africa and telling him that he grew up near Bregenz at Lake Constance. The colleague is unable to understand such a thing. "I have been there, too; I know that place! How can anyone move away from the most beautiful place in the world?"

And the anecdote told in a pub in Vorarlberg is also hard to forget. A visitor listens for a while to the stories about America told by a local. Finally, the visitor risks asking the local how long the teller of the story had been living in the USA. "Me, why me? I'm talking about my brother, he always wanted to emigrate ...".

Well, there are always picture books, so that homesick people from Vorarlberg can always carry a piece of their homeland around with them.

Besiedelte Landschaft. Zwei Drittel der Einwohner des Bundeslandes Vorarlberg – also rund 240.000 Menschen – wohnen im Rheintal, das sich vom Bodensee bis zur Stadt Feldkirch erstreckt. Trotz dieser dichten Besiedelung zeigt der Blick vom Gebhardsberg ob Bregenz zwischen den abendlich erleuchteten Siedlungsgebieten und Straßenbändern dunkelgrüne Flecken. Die Landespolitik setzt darauf, Grünzonen wie die Riedlandschaften zu erhalten, als Lebensraum für die seltene Tier- und Pflanzenwelt ebenso wie als Naherholungsgebiete und Landwirtschaftsflächen. Nutzungskonflikte sind vorprogrammiert, besonders bei Straßenbauprojekten.

A colonised landscape. Two thirds of the total population of the Austrian state of Vorarlberg - around 240,000 people - live in the Rheintal (Rhine Valley), which stretches from Lake Constance to the town of Feldkirch. Despite such a population density, large areas of dark green remain clearly visible between the night lights of the settlements and roads on this view from Gebhardsberg, above Bregenz. Local policy insists on the preservation of green areas such as the reed landscapes as habitat for rare species of animal and plant, as local places of recreation and for farming. Conflicts of interest regarding land use are a way of life here, especially when new roads are planned.

Wanderern und Bikern ist es vorbehalten, auf der Alpe Gsohl oberhalb der Stadt Hohenems zuzukehren. Von Mai bis Oktober wird dort auf 980 m gewirtet. Wer lange genug ausharrt, den mag diese Abendstimmung verabschieden, wenn Sonne und aufsteigender Bodennebel miteinander wetteifern und sich die Sonne schließlich für einige Stunden zurückzieht.

Hikers and mountain bikers are advised to take a detour to Alp Gsohl above the town of Hohenems. From May to October, a café opens here which is situated at 980 m, and those who stay long enough into the evening are often able to enjoy the views of the ascending ground fog competing with the sun and to watch the sun slowly set over a few hours.

Mit der Fünf-Tage-Woche hat die Landwirtschaft nichts am Hut, weder am Bauernhof noch auf der Alpe. Es braucht Begeisterung für die Arbeit, deren Ergebnis – beste Milch, Butter und Käse – von Feinschmeckern sehr geschätzt wird. Die Pflege der Landschaft durch weidende Kühe ist wohl ebenso wichtig. Nicht mehr bewirtschaftete Alpen wachsen rasch mit Büschen und Bäumen zu. Fast ein Viertel der Landesfläche, insgesamt 62.000 Hektar, umfassen die Alpen im Land und etwa 40.000 Stück Vieh werden gealpt, davon rund 9.500 Milchkühe.

Farming in this area has is not merely a 'Monday to Friday job' - neither at the farmhouse nor in the hills. It requires enthusiasm and dedication, the results of which - best quality milk, butter and cheese - are treasured by gourmands. The nurturing of the land by grazing cows is also very important. Abandoned Alpine pastures rapidly become overgrown with undergrowth and trees. The alpine pastures account for almost a quarter of the land in Vorarlberg, or 62,000 hectares in total, and around 40,000 units of livestock are grazed, of which 9,500 are dairy cows.

Eine der 137 Alpen in Vorarlberg, auf denen noch gesennt wird, wo also Käse entsteht, ist die Metzgertobel Alpe oberhalb von Buchboden im Großen Walsertal.
Die Produktion im Land ist beeindruckend: Vorarlberg erzeugt rund 460.000 Kilogramm Alpkäse, dazu kommen 80.000 kg „Sura Kees", eine Spezialität im Montafon. Vorarlberger Alpkäse darf nur heißen, was tatsächlich aus naturbelassener Milch von Alpvieh erzeugt wird. Das Verfahren wurde erstmals während des Dreißigjährigen Krieges, also in der ersten Hälfte des 17. Jahrhunderts, beschrieben. Im mit Holz beheizten Kupferkessel wird die Milch erhitzt, Lab sorgt dafür, dass die Milch bricht. Senn Leo Türtscher holt den Käsebruch mit einem Käsetuch aus dem Kessel.

One of the 137 alpine pastures in Vorarlberg at which cheese is produced is the Metzgertobel pasture above Buchboden in the Great Walser Valley.
The levels of output in the state are impressive: Vorarlberg produces around 460,000 kilograms of alpine cheese as well as 80,000 kg of ‚Sura Kees' cheese, a speciality in Montafon. Only cheeses which are produced using naturally processed milk from alpine cattle is permitted to be called Vorarlberg alpine cheese. The procedure was first described during the thirty year war, in the first half of the 17th century. The milk is heated in a copper tank, rennet ensures that the milk curdles. Dairyman Leo Türscher removes the cheese curd from the tank with a cheese cloth.

Käselaibe wollen gepflegt werden. Mindestens 3 Monate benötigt Alpkäse zur Reifung, nach mindestens 6 Monaten wird der Käse pikant. In dieser Zeit werden die etwa 35 kg schweren Laibe regelmäßig gebürstet und mit Salzlauge gewaschen.

Loaves of cheese have to be treated with care. Alpine cheese requires at least 3 months to mature and the cheese only gains its flavour after at least 6 months. During this time, the 35 kg heavy cheese loaves are regularly brushed down and washed with brine.

Viele der Vorarlberger Bauern sind auch heute noch Teilzeitnomaden. Ende Mai, Anfang Juni übersiedelt die Familie vom Hof im Tal auf das Maisäß oder Vorsäß, eine Art Niederalm, wobei der Ausdruck „Alm" in Vorarlberg gar nicht gut ankommt, weil hierzulande eben „Alpe" heißt, was andernorts mit „Alm" bezeichnet wird. Im Sommer geht es dann auf die Hochalpe, 560 davon sind in Vorarlberg noch bestoßen, also bewirtschaftet. Natürlich sind die Älpler oft mit Traktor und Geländefahrzeug unterwegs, manche Alpe ist aber nur zu Fuß und mit dem Saumpferd erreichbar. Hier geht es auf die Oberalp in Hintermellen im Gemeindegebiet von Hohenems.

Many of the farmers in the Vorarlberg remain part time nomads to this day. At the end of May and start of June, the family migrates from their farm in the valley to their 'Maisäß' or 'Vorsäß' farm, a kind of lower Alm (alpine pasture). The word 'Alm', however, isn't really used in Vorarlberg so much, as in this region the word 'Alp' is used to describe that which is elsewhere called 'Alm'. In the summer, the ascent to the 'Hochalpe' (high alpine pasture) is then made, of which 560 are still farmed in Vorarlberg. The alpine farmers are often to be seen on the move and at work in cross country vehicles and tractors - but some alpine pastures remain only accessible by foot and with pack horse. This view shows the upper alpine area of Hintermellen in the commune of Hohenems.

SEITE 26/27
Der lange Marsch von der Alpe ins Tal lässt die Leiber der Rinder richtig dampfen, hier auf der Bregenzerwälder Bundesstraße beim Marsch in den Himmelriese-Tunnel zwischen Schröcken und Schoppernau.

The long march from the alpine pasture into the valley really makes the cattle sweat, as shown here on the main Bregenz Forest road marching in the Himmelriese tunnel between Schröcken and Schoppernau.

Der Alpabtrieb Mitte September ist ein wichtiges Ereignis im bäuerlichen Jahreskreis und längst auch für viele Besucher eine Attraktion. Verlief die Alpsaison unfallfrei, sind nicht nur Hirtenbuben, Sennerinnen und Senner geschmückt, sondern auch das Vieh. Hier kommt ein Alpabtrieb über die Hochbrücke zwischen Bersbuch und Schwarzenberg im Vorderen Bregenzerwald.

The 'Alpabtrieb', or alpine descent - the bringing of the cattle down from the alpine pastures - in mid September is an important date in the agricultural calendar and has long since been an attraction for visitors. If the alpine season was free of accidents then shepherd boys, shepherds and livestock are all decorated. This view shows an alpine descent procession over the high bridge between Bersbuch and Schwarzenberg before the Bregenz Forest.

Alpabtrieb und Alptag in Schwarzenberg. Hier werden die Kühe wieder ihren Besitzern übergeben, hier begutachten und prämieren Fachleute auch den Alpkäse. Der Andrang ist groß auf dem Dorfplatz, der als der schönste weitum gilt, gesäumt von prachtvollen Wirtshäusern und der Kirche mit Werken von Angelika Kauffmann, die ihre Wurzeln in Schwarzenberg hatte.

Alpine descent and Alpine day in Schwarzenberg. Here, the cows are returned to their owners, experts also test and award prizes to the alpine cheeses. Crowds gather at the village square, one of the most beautiful in the region, fringed by splendid looking inns and the church that contains works by Angelika Kauffmann, who had her roots in Schwarzenberg.

Bezau
Warth
Egg
Bregenz
Egg

„'s Wäldarbähle macht a Ränkle", heißt es in einem beliebten Vorarlberger Lied und das will heißen, dass die Bregenzerwaldbahn eine Kurve fährt. Sie tut es wieder, nachdem der Betrieb der Schmalspurbahn von Bregenz nach Bezau im Bregenzerwald 1985 nach 83 Betriebsjahren eingestellt worden war. Jetzt betreibt ein Verein die Museumsbahn auf verkürzter Strecke von Bezau bis Schwarzenberg mit liebevoll restaurierten Dampflokomotiven und Waggons.

"'s Wäldarbähle macht a Ränkle", lyrics to a popular Vorarlberg folk song which means 'the Bregenz Forest railway is taking a curve'. And that's something it now does once more since the reopening of the narrow gauge railway from Bregenz to Bezau in the Bregenz forest, originally closed after 83 years of operation in 1985. An association is now running the heritage line on a shortened route from Bezau to Schwarzenberg with lovingly restored steam locomotives and wagons.

Dafür leistet die Taurus am Arlberg Schwerstarbeit. Die 86 t schwere Lok der ÖBB (Österreichische Bundesbahnen) bewährt sich im Eisenbahnverkehr durch den Arlberg, lange Zeit die einzige wintersichere Verbindung zwischen Vorarlberg und Tirol.

The 'Taurus' works especially hard on the Arlberg. The 86 ton ÖBB locomotive (Austrian Railways) has proved its worth time and again on the railway journey through the Arlberg, for a long time the only winter's connection between Vorarlberg and the Tyrol.

Wenn im Herbst Nebelschwaden über das Ried ziehen, erhält die Landschaft ein besonderes Gesicht, die Masten der Hochspannungsleitungen scheinen sich wie in einem Traum zu verflüchtigen. Sie ermöglichen den Export von Spitzenstrom aus den Wasserkraftwerken, mit eine Basis für den Wohlstand in Vorarlberg. Davor ein Acker mit „Türggo", wie Mais in Vorarlberg in Anlehnung an den alten Begriff „Türkenkorn" heute noch heißt. Der daraus erzeugte „Riebel" war einst tägliche Kost für viele Familien. Dass die heimische Bussi-Bussi- und Adabei-Gesellschaft inzwischen das einstige Arme-Leute-Essen

entdeckt hat und es an Events als vermeintlich rare Spezialität zelebriert und serviert, hat sich wohl nicht vermeiden lassen.

When the mists waft over the reeds in the autumn, the landscape gains a special appearance, and the electricity cable masts seem to disappear into the mist. These lines facilitate the export of peak current electricity from the hydroelectric power stations, making an important contribution to the prosperity of Vorarlberg. In the foreground, a field of 'Türggo'. This word which is still used to designate maize in Vorarlberg and cognate with the old expression of 'Türkenkorn' or 'Turkish corn'. The 'Riebel' porridge which is produced from this once formed the daily diet of many families. To the regret of some, this dish, once the preserve of the poor, has recently been discovered and 're-branded' by the young and upwardly mobile, and is now served as a rare local speciality at events and parties.

Strom aus Wasserkraft ist Vorarlbergs „weißes Gold", pro Jahr erzeugen heimische Kraftwerke über 3.000 Mio. kWh an sauberer Energie. Die großen Speicherkraftwerke von Illwerke-VKW liefern den gefragten Spitzenstrom, der bei Bedarf innert Sekunden zur Verfügung steht, auch an ausländische Partner. Bild links: Das Turbinenhaus im 1957 eröffneten Lünersee-Kraftwerk, einem bedeutsamen Mosaikstein der Energieversorgung im Land. Vor 50 Jahren war es mit seinem Regelarbeitsvermögen von 371 Mio. kWh das größte Pumpspeicherkraftwerk der Welt.

Hydroelectric power is Vorarlberg's white gold: the local power stations produce more than 3,000 million kWh of clean electrical energy each year. The large 'Illwerke-VKW' storage power stations produce the peak current electricity which, if necessary, can be made available within seconds, to both domestic and international partners. Image, left: the turbine house at the Lünersee power station which opened in 1957, an Austrian milestone in the production of electricity. When the plant opened 50 years ago, its average output of 371 million kWh made it the biggest pumped storage hydro power station in the world.

Eine etwas andere Energie durch Wasserkraft nutzen auch die Wildholzer am Bodensee und an den Ufern von Rhein und Bregenzerache. Bei Hochwässern nach Gewitterregen trägt das Wasser Energie in Form von Holz durch die Flussläufe Richtung See. Von den Dämmen der Flüsse aus oder im See wird das wertvolle Brennmaterial geborgen. Der erfahrene Holzer Walter Loitz hat am Seeufer im Gaißauer Rheinholz Ernte gehalten, mit seinem robusten Puch-Moped wird die Fracht auf dem Anhänger heimgeführt.

The lumberjacks make use of a different kind of water energy at Lake Constance and on the banks of the Rhein and Bregenzer Ach rivers. When the river waters are high after heavy rainfalls, they carry energy in the form of fallen wood and timber towards the lake. This valuable fuel is then salvaged at the river dams or in the lake. Experienced lumberjack Walter Loitz has gathered some Rhine timber at the lakeside in Gaißau. With his powerful Puch moped and trailer, he transports his cargo home.

BAUR
TG 20/50

Vom Agrarland über das Textilland zum Land mit anspruchsvoller technischer Entwicklung und Produktion – und dennoch nach wie vor beliebtes Urlaubsland. Vorarlberg weiß die unterschiedlichen Anforderungen in Einklang zu bringen, weil dem Schutz der Umwelt großes Augenmerk gilt. Vorarlberg verfügt nicht über Bodenschätze, dennoch führen Metallwaren und elektronische Produkte die Exportstatistik an. Sie haben längst die früher dominierenden Textilien abgelöst. Das schafft zusätzlich zu den hohen Erlösen auch gefragte Arbeitsplätze.

An agricultural region, a textiles region, a region noted for its high quality technical developments and production - and as ever, a popular holiday region. Vorarlberg knows the importance of reconciling the different requirements, especially since protecting the environment is considered imperative. Vorarlberg doesn't boast mineral resources; its primary exports are metal goods and electronic goods, the production of which has long replaced once dominant textiles industry. Along with solid company earnings, this also creates high value employment.

Dem Druck der Billigkonkurrenz aus Fernost haben viele der einstigen Flaggschiffe der Vorarlberger Textilindustrie nicht standhalten können, immer wieder gab es Betriebsschließungen. Am Markt zu behaupten wissen sich einige ausgesuchte Betriebe, die statt Massenware besonders hochwertige Erzeugnisse liefern. Dazu gehört die Getzner Textil AG in Bludenz. Modische und technische Spitzenleistungen sowie enge Zusammenarbeit mit internationalen Modegrößen bescheren dem Weber und Textilveredler erfreulich gut gefüllte Auftragsbücher. Rasch, verlässlich und flexibel zu sein, sind Voraussetzungen dafür. Auch Sticker und Stricker im Land, die auf Luxusproduktion setzen, haben kaum Absatzprobleme. Die Nachfrage nach Qualität ist ungebrochen.

Over the years, many flagship companies in the Vorarlberg textiles industry have been unable to survive the pressure caused by low cost competition from the Far East. Closures were commonplace. The few niche companies which remain have focused on the manufacturing of high quality, specialist products rather than mass production. One of these companies is Getzner Textil AG in Bludenz. Top quality couture and technical services as well as close collaboration with international fashion giants ensure the order books of this particular weaving and textiles business remain full. Being fast, reliable and flexible are all necessary for survival in the market. Weavers and knitters who focus on luxury products appear to experience few business problems as well. The demand for quality remains unbroken.

DEMAG
2t
KS115
KS080
KS075
KS074

Höchste Qualität zeichnet auch die wachsende Zahl der Metallverarbeiter in Vorarlberg aus. Vom hoch spezialisierten Ein-Mann-Betrieb bis zum weltweit aktiven Konzern mit Milliardenumsatz ist hier alles zu finden. Blum Beschläge in Höchst (im Bild das Werk 5) hat sich aus einer kleinen Schmiede zum Familienunternehmen mit über 5.000 Mitarbeiterinnen und Mitarbeitern entwickelt. 97 % des Umsatzes werden außerhalb Österreichs gemacht.

The growing number of metal processing businesses in Vorarlberg is also noted for their high quality products and services. From highly specialist 'one man' operations to international corporations with turnovers that run into the billions - everything can be found here. The company Blum hardware in Höchst (factory 5 pictured) has developed from a small smithy to a family firm which employs more than 5,000 workers. 97 % of its revenues are generated outside Austria.

Sinnvolle Nachnutzung ist angesagt beim Wandel, den Vorarlbergs Industrielandschaft während der vergangenen Jahrzehnte durchgemacht hat. Da siedelt der Skihersteller in der einstigen Textilfabrik, es entstehen Gewerbeparks mit flexiblem Platzangebot für aufstrebende Jungunternehmer. Zusätzlich wird in attraktiver Lage Grund frei für Wohnbau, der sich erfreulich abhebt von manchen der Wohnsilos, die vor wenigen Jahrzehnten errichtet worden sind. Sowohl private Bauträger als auch gemeinnützige Gesellschaften setzen im Wohnbau auf Qualität und auf energiebewusste Bauweise. Im Bild rechts: Wohnbauten vor dem Gewerbepark „Rhomberg's Fabrik", einem der einst großen Dornbirner Textilunternehmen, vor dem Hintergrund der Parzelle Haselstauder Berg. Bild oben: das Otten-Areal in Hohenems, ebenfalls ein zum Gewerbepark und Veranstaltungszentrum gewandelter Textilbetrieb.

Meaningful re-use has featured strongly in the period of change through which Vorarlberg's industrial areas have gone through in recent decades. Ski manufacturers have made former textile factories their home, business parks have emerged offering flexible space to young companies and new business start ups. Space has also become available for the construction of homes, which are thankfully of a higher standard than the soulless housing estates constructed in decades past. Both private property developers and public housing organizations insist on quality and energy efficiency with their housing. The image on the right shows residential buildings in front of the 'Rhomberg's Fabrik' business park, once home to one of the biggest textile businesses in Dornbirn, before the background of the Haselstauder mountain region. The image above shows the Otten Areal in Hohenems, also a business park exhibition centre which has been built on the site of a former textiles factory.

Unternehmenskultur in Vorarlberg. „Ja klar, der darf das!" So meinten nicht wenige, als direkt hinter dem alten Schmied-Rohner Haus in Höchst im Rheindelta ein neues Verwaltungsgebäude des größten Unternehmens im Ort in die Höhe wuchs. Das ganze Grundstück samt Wohnhaus gehört längst dem Unternehmen Blum Beschläge, die Erben haben es verkauft. Die frühere Besitzerin, die das Häuschen seit mehr als 50 Jahren bewohnt, wollte aber lieber nicht übersiedeln. Das darf kein Problem sein, entschied die Unternehmensleitung: Die betagte, rüstige Frau bleibt eben in dem Haus, so lang sie das wünscht. Und dann wurde das Häuschen auf Kosten des Unternehmens noch ein wenig renoviert – es soll ja ein Gesicht haben, das eigenwillige Ensemble.

Die Entscheidung auf dem Bild rechts hingegen traf allein die Natur, nachdem allerdings der Mensch durch Kahlschlag gegen Ende des 18. Jahrhunderts den Anstoß gegeben hatte: Im Schesatobel, dem größten Murbruch in den Ostalpen, sind über 40 Millionen Kubikmeter Material abgetragen worden. Das Bauernhaus auf dem Hang in Bürs bei Bludenz im Walgau ist allerdings nicht gefährdet. Nur die fotografische Perspektive rückt es so nahe an den Murbruch, da liegt noch ausreichend viel stabiler Boden bis zum Abhang. Und die Sicherungsmaßnahmen, die vor über 100 Jahren gestartet worden sind, bewähren sich.

Business culture in Vorarlberg. "Go right ahead!" Such were the thoughts of more than just a few people when construction of a new administrative building for the largest company in the town started directly behind the old Schmied-Rohner house (metal workers' house) in Höchst, at the Rhine delta. The whole plot of land together with the residential building has long belonged to the company Blum Beschläge, to whom it was sold by the heirs. The previous owner, who lived in the house for more than 50 years, didn't want to move though. The company management decided that this wasn't a problem: the sprightly old lady was able to stay in the house as long as she wanted. The house was then renovated a little at the company's expense - the outlandish ensemble is to have a face.

The decision on the right hand image was taken by nature alone, however, after the impetus brought about by man-made deforestation towards the end of the 18th century: In Schesatobel, the largest mud slide in the eastern Alps, more than 40 million cubic meters of material has been removed. The farmhouse on the slope in Bürs bei Bludenz in the Walgau is not in danger, however. It is only the photographic perspective which makes it seem so close to the mud slide. There is actually sufficient stable ground until the precipice. And the securing measures which were originally started more than 100 years ago are proving sufficient.

Bergbahnstationen müssen keineswegs aussehen wie missglückte Bergkirchlein. Ebenso wie die alten Heustadel und Vorsäßhütten im Montafon versteckt die Mittelstation der Golmerbahn auf Matschwitz ihre Funktion nicht. Transparent und markant ragt sie auf, beeindruckt und überzeugt. Wie etliche der Aufstiegshilfen im Montafon hat die Golmerbahn ihren Ursprung als Transportbahn beim Bau von Stauseen oder Druckleitungen des Stromerzeugers Illwerke. Am Golm oberhalb von Tschagguns begann die Personenbeförderung im Jahr 1959. Aus dem einstigen Schrägaufzug wurde eine moderne Einseilumlaufbahn mit 8er-Kabinen.

Cable car stations don't have to look like imitation mountain chapels. Just like the old hay barns and lower mountain pasture huts in Montafon, the middle station of the Golmerbahn refuses to hide its functionality, towering transparently and proudly with an impressive and convincing sense of purpose. As many of the climbing aids in Montafon, the original purpose of the Golmerbahn was to assist in transportation during the construction of reservoirs and in pressure lines for the Illwerke power plant. The transportation of people at Golm above Tschagguns began in 1959. The former funicular railway was converted into a modern cable railway with cabins that hold 8 people.

Wer von Schuttannen im Gemeindegebiet Hohenems Richtung Fluhereck wandert, der stößt am Fuß des Wendkopfes auf die Alpe Hinterberg (Bild links), winters wie sommers ein lohnenswerter Ausflug. Auch unmittelbar neben einer viel befahrenen Skipiste ist unberührter Winterzauber möglich, wie dieser verschneite Stadel bei der Abfahrt vom Kriegerhorn in Lech zeigt (rechts).

Those who walk from Schuttannen in the commune of Hohenems towards Fluhereck eventually reach the Hinterberg alpine pasture in the foothills of the Wendkopf, a worthwhile excursion in both summer and winter. Magical winter views are also possible in the proximity of much used skiing slopes, as shown by this snowy barn on leaving the Kriegerhorn in Lech (right).

Wer von Schuttannen im Gemeindegebiet Hohenems Richtung Fluhereck wandert, der stößt am Fuß des Wendkopfes auf die Alpe Hinterberg (Bild links), winters wie sommers ein lohnenswerter Ausflug. Auch unmittelbar neben einer viel befahrenen Skipiste ist unberührter Winterzauber möglich, wie dieser verschneite Stadel bei der Abfahrt vom Kriegerhorn in Lech zeigt (rechts).

Those who walk from Schuttannen in the commune of Hohenems towards Fluhereck eventually reach the Hinterberg alpine pasture in the foothills of the Wendkopf, a worthwhile excursion in both summer and winter. Magical winter views are also possible in the proximity of much used skiing slopes, as shown by this snowy barn on leaving the Kriegerhorn in Lech (right).

SEITE 52 / 53
Winterliches Dornbirn. Vorarlbergs Wirtschafts-Hauptstadt hat sich in ihrem Zentrum alte Bürger- und Geschäftshäuser bewahrt und bietet zu jeder Jahreszeit ein einladendes Bild.

Dornbirn in the winter. The commercial capital of Vorarlberg boasts an impressive selection of well preserved town houses and commercial buildings and is an attractive town in all seasons.

SEITE 54 / 55
Hohenems, die jüngste Stadt Vorarlbergs mit großer Geschichte. Wuchtig der alte Palast der Emser Grafen unter dem Stadtschrofen, inzwischen im Besitz der Grafen von Waldburg-Zeil und beliebter Raum für Kulturveranstaltungen. Die Stadt war lange Jahrhunderte auch ein Zentrum jüdischen Lebens im Land.

Hohenems, the youngest town in Vorarlberg - but with an impressive past. Situated beneath the town cliffs, the old palace of the counts of Ems is an impressive sight. It is now in the ownership of the counts of Waldburg-Zeil and a popular location for cultural events. For several centuries, this town was also the centre of Jewish life in the region.

DORNBIRNER
SPAR

Sagmeister

Die mittelalterliche Oberstadt von Bregenz, gefasst vom Martinsturm mit seiner markanten Zwiebelkuppel und dem Gourmettempel Deuringschlössle, wurde gegen Ende des 12. Jahrhunderts gegründet und im darauf folgenden Jahrhundert stark befestigt. Der Martinsturm selbst entstand auf dem ehemaligen Getreidespeicher der Grafen von Bregenz. Nach wie vor ist die Oberstadt ein Hort der Ruhe.

The medieval upper town of Bregenz, with the Martinsturm and its striking dome and the Deuringschlössle hotel and restaurant complex, was established towards the end of the 12th century and fortified over the following century. The Martinsturm itself was built on the former grain store belonging to the counts of Bregenz. As always, the upper town remains a place of tranquillity.

Aus den traurigen Resten der Burg Hohenbregenz über der Landeshauptstadt ist inzwischen das Ausflugs- und Wallfahrtsziel Gebhardsberg geworden. In der Burg soll 949 der hl. Gebhard geboren worden sein, der spätere Bischof von Konstanz. Ihm ist die Kapelle in der Burgruine geweiht, mehr Besucher registriert wohl das Burgrestaurant Gebhardsberg.

The remnants of Hohenbregenz castle above the state capital is now the Gebhardsberg excursion and pilgrimage destination. St. Gebhard was supposedly born here in the year 949, later the Bishop of Konstanz. The chapel in the castle ruins is consecrated in his name, although the castle restaurant of Gebhardsberg attracts more visitors.

Der markante Feldkircher Edelsitz „Schloss Amberg" soll um 1493 von Kaiser Maximilian I. für seine Geliebte Anna von Helfenstein errichtet worden sein. Sie vererbte es dem gemeinsamen Sohn Max Friedrich von Amberg (1511-1553). Inzwischen in Privatbesitz, steht das Schloss samt Garten für kulturelle Veranstaltungen oder Hochzeiten und Seminare offen.

The impressive Feldkircher seat of nobility, castle Amberg, was built around 1493 by Kaiser Maximilian I for his beloved Anna von Helfenstein. It was inherited by their son, Max Friedrich von Amberg (1511-1553). Now in private ownership, the castle and its gardens are available for weddings and seminars and also host cultural events.

Der Eingang zum Walgau wird wie einst von der Stadt Feldkirch bewacht, welche in der Neustadt und Marktgasse ein besonders gut erhaltenes mittelalterliches Stadtbild aufweist. Über der Stadt ragt die Schattenburg auf, einst Stammsitz der Grafen von Montfort. Ihr Banner ist heute Wappen des Bundeslandes Vorarlberg. Feldkirch ist auch Bischofssitz, hier finden sich Landesgericht, Landeskonservatorium und pädagogische Hochschule.

The entrance to Walgau remains, as always, watched over by the town of Feldkirch, which boasts a particularly well preserved medieval townscape, especially in the Neustadt and the Marktgasse. Schattenburg castle towers above the town, once the seat of the counts of Montfort. Their banner is now the coat of arms of the Federal State of Vorarlberg. Feldkirch is also the bishop's see, and home to the state courts, the state conservatorium and the college of education.

Funde aus der frühen Bronzezeit gegen 2.000 v.Chr. belegen, dass die Stadt Bludenz im Walgau bereits früh als Siedlungsort gefragt gewesen ist. Das Bezirksstädtchen nutzte später die Vorteile der Lage am Schnittpunkt von Walgau, Brandnertal, Montafon und Klostertal und war Ausgangspunkt für Reisen über den Arlberg. Nach wie vor ist der Bahnhof Bludenz Vorarlberger Angelpunkt für die Arlbergbahn. Das Bild zeigt im Vordergrund den Turm der Laurentiuskirche, hinter der Häuserzeile das Bahnhofsgelände sowie dann den Blick zur Nachbargemeinde Bürs und den Eingang zur Bürser Schlucht. Eindrucksvoll das einstige Spinnereigebäude der Lünerseefabrik, heute ein Gewerbepark mit vorgelagertem Einkaufszentrum.

Findings from the early Bronze Age around 2,000 BC prove that the town of Bludenz in Walgau has been a settlement since ancient times. The county town then benefited the advantages of its location at the hub of the Walgau, Brandner, Montafon and Kloster valleys and as a starting point for excursions over the Arlberg. As previously Bludenz station is the Vorarlberg hub for the Arlberg railway. In the foreground of the image we have the tower of the Laurentius church, behind the row of houses, the railway station area, and then the view towards the neighbouring commune of Bürs and the inlet to the Bürs gorge. The former spinning mill buildings of the Lünersee factory, today a business park and shopping centre, are also impressive.

Zwei Walserinnen aus Sonntag im großen Walsertal, unterwegs in ihrer traditionellen Tracht mit der „Brämchappa", der Kopfbedeckung aus Seehundfell.

Two Walser women from Sonntag in the Great Walser Valley, wearing traditional costume including the 'Brämchappa', a headdress made from seal skin.

KULTUR UND BRAUCHTUM CULTURES AND TRADITIONS

Die beiden jüngeren Begleiterinnen des Walser Mannes auf dem Bild links oben tragen das „Schäppili". Dieser den jungen Frauen vorbehaltene Kopfputz ist aus Silberfäden, Gold- und Silberplättchen und Glasperlen geformt. Bild links unten: Das „Schappale" der Tracht der Bregenzerwälderin ist breiter, geformt wie ein Kelch und goldfarben. Auch dieser Kopfschmuck wird nur bis zum Tag der Hochzeit getragen. Was heimische Trachtenkapellen tragen, ist eher zeitgemäß geschnitten und erinnert nur entfernt an die originalen Trachten von einst. Viele der 123 Musikvereine im Land marschieren auch in Uniformen aus. Ohne sie ist ein zünftiges Fest in Vorarlberg kaum vorstellbar.

The two younger escorts to the Walser gentleman in the image on the left are wearing the 'Schäppili', however. Image bottom left: The headdress designated for younger women with silver threading, gold and silver lamella and glass pearls. The 'Shappale', the traditional ladies headdress in the Bregenz Forest region, is wider, chalice shaped and gold in colour. This is only worn until marriage. The costumes worn by the marching bands without whom an appropriate party is almost inconceivable, have a more contemporary cut than the original costumes. Many of the region's 123 music associations march in their own uniforms.

An Feiertagen und Festlichkeiten oder auch, wenn ein geachteter Mitbürger zu Grabe getragen wird, dann trifft der Besucher im Großen Walsertal, im Montafon oder im Bregenzerwald auf Einheimische in der Tracht der Talschaft, selbstverständlich noch fein abgestuft je nach Wohnort. Besonders farbenprächtig ist die Tracht im Großen Walsertal. Besiedelt wurde das Tal im 14. Jahrhundert durch Bauern, die aus dem Schweizer Wallis in das Gebiet vor dem Arlberg zogen. Die Ursachen für die alpine Völkerwanderung liegen im Dunkeln, es gibt unterschiedliche Erklärungen: von Hungersnot im Wallis bis zu Söldnertum für die damaligen Herren im Gebiet Vorarlberg.

Ebenso wie andere bäuerliche Trachten bildete sich die der Walser erst im 18. und 19. Jahrhundert in der bis heute bestehenden Form heraus. Man war jemand und zeigte das auch.

Erfreulich aktiv präsentiert sich das Große Walsertal heute. Nach dem Grundsatz: „Die Natur nutzen, ohne ihr zu schaden", gehen die Talbewohner rücksichtsvoll um mit dem, was heute Ressource genannt wird, was sie aber als schützenswerte Heimat empfinden. Gerade einmal 3.500 Menschen leben in den sechs Walser Gemeinden und sanfter Tourismus ist hier kein Schlagwort, sondern gelebter Alltag. So erkannte im Jahr 2000 die UNESCO das Tal als Biosphärenpark an. Ob bewusste Holznutzung, Verwertung von Kräutern oder besonderes Käseangebot – hier sind bäuerliche Kultur und Brauchtum eng miteinander verwoben. Wen wundert's, dass ein beliebter Exportartikel aus dem Tal, ein Bergkäse, den Namen „Walserstolz" trägt?

Dass im Tal erfolgreiche Handwerksbetriebe zu finden sind und auch Firmen aus dem High-Tech-Bereich, das verwundert nicht: Auch ein Computerspezialist arbeitet gern mit Ausblick auf eine schonend genutzte Natur. Und zum nächsten Flughafen dauert die Fahrt kaum länger als in einer Großstadt.

On public holidays, during celebrations, or when a respected local citizen is laid to rest, visitors to the Great Walser Valley, Montafon or the Bregenz Forest will see local residents dressed in their traditional costumes, with the degree of finery varying according to location. The traditional dress in the Great Walser Valley is especially colourful. The valley was settled by farmers in the 14th century who moved from Wallis in Switzerland to the area before the Arlberg. The reasons behind the migration are uncertain and there are differing explanations, such as a supposed famine in Wallis, or the mercenary armies of the era which attracted men to the Vorarlberg region.

The traditional agrarian costumes of the Walser people took their current shape in the 18th and 19th centuries. They were people of a certain standing, and they liked to show it.

The Great Walser Valley is a refreshingly active place nowadays. According to the motto 'protecting nature without damaging it' residents of the valley take a responsible approach to that which is often called a resource but what they view as being their home, and worthy of protection. Little more than 3,500 people live in the six communes of Walser, and 'responsible tourism' here isn't simply a slogan, it is an everyday reality. It is in this sense that UNESCO identified the valley as a biosphere park in the year 2000. Whether it is the responsible use of wood, the utilisation of herbs or specialist cheeses, farming cultures and traditions are woven closely together here. Who should be surprised that a popular export item from the valley, a mountain cheese, has the name 'Walserstolz' - the 'pride of Walser'?

The fact that successful craft businesses are also located in the valley along with high tech companies shouldn't be so surprising: computer specialists also enjoy working with views over natural surroundings that are used in a way which is sustainable. And the journey to the nearest airport is little longer than that from a suburb to a city centre.

Ganz genau kontrolliert Abfindungsbrenner Robert Humpeler in Fußach am Bodensee, ob beim Schnapsbrennen alles seine Ordnung hat. Sorgfältig hat der Zimmermann im Ruhestand im Herbst die geernteten Früchte gemahlen und zu Maische verarbeitet. Jetzt brennt er, unterstützt von Sohn Herbert, auf dem Vorplatz seines Hauses einen edlen Tropfen mit der fahrbaren Schnapsbrennerei des Obst- und Gartenbauvereines Höchst.

Fußach am Bodensee: authorized distiller Robert Humpeler checks whether everything is in order when distilling schnapps. The retired carpenter carefully ground the harvested fruits in autumn, making them into a mash, and with the help of his son Herbert, he now distils a premium drop in the courtyard of his house with the portable schnapps distillery of the Höchst fruit and market gardening association.

Leutscheu

Wer hierzulande aufwächst, bekommt immer wieder zu hören, der typische Vorarlberger sei verschlossen und „leutscheu", meide also den Kontakt mit Menschen, die er nicht kennt. Diese Sorte an Vorarlbergern ist gewiss noch zu finden, die „Leutscheuen" bilden aber inzwischen wohl eine Minderheit. Da sind viel mehr solche anzutreffen, die mit allen und jedem gleich per Du sind, die herzlich einladen und zu erzählen beginnen. Gäste zeigen sich erstaunt: „Wenn wir spazieren gehen, dann grüßt uns jeder. Ich kenne die Leute doch gar nicht, warum machen die das?"

Das mit dem eigenbrötlerischen Vorarlberger ist also wohl eher Vergangenheit. Deshalb kann auch, wer in ein Dorf in Vorarlberg zieht, nach wenigen Monaten eine freundliche Einladung ihm völlig fremder Menschen erhalten, die nicht einmal etwas verkaufen möchten. „Liebe Jahrgängerin, lieber Jahrgänger!" ist da zu lesen. Manche dieser Jahrgängergruppen sind bestens organisiert, es gibt regelmäßig gemeinsame Veranstaltungen, andere bescheiden sich mit einem Ausflug pro Jahr oder zu runden Geburtstagen. Jedenfalls bietet sich neu Zugezogenen die Chance, rasch mit Gleichaltrigen Bekanntschaft zu schließen.

Der Kultur-Alemanne

Der Spruch vom Alemannen, der nicht singe und sich kaum für Kultur interessiere – abgesehen vielleicht von Ländler und Marschmusik – ist ebenfalls längst Geschichte. Niemand hat heute auch nur die geringste Chance, all die zahllosen Kulturtermine wahrzunehmen, die sich allenthalben und an allen Tagen des Jahres anbieten. Darunter gibt es gefragte Perlen wie die Schubertiade in Hohenems und Schwarzenberg, die Bregenzer Festspiele, die selbst James Bond zu einem Besuch verlocken konnten, und eine Vielzahl wertvoller Kulturinitiativen von traditionsbewusst bis provokant modern.

Er singt, der Alemanne, und er musiziert, ob in Musical-Produktionen oder Opernaufführungen, in Hausmusikgruppen und Orchestern. Selbstverständlich spielt er auch Theater, voller Begeisterung, vom Bauernschwank bis zur Umsetzung besonders anspruchsvoller Bühnenstücke. Brauchtum und Kultur sind auch verbunden mit den 123 Vorarlberger Blaskapellen – eine stolze Zahl bei insgesamt 96 Gemeinden.
Ein Kunsthaus wie das am Hafen von Bregenz muss sich ein kleines Land erst leisten und die Heimatmuseen haben die Spinnweben längst von Mistgabeln und Butterfässern gefegt. Ob Frauenmuseum Hittisau, Jüdisches Museum Hohenems, Textildruckmuseum Hard, Rhein-Schauen Lustenau, Bergbaumuseum Silbertal, Walsermuseum Riezlern/Kleinwalsertal – die Liste ist beeindruckend und natürlich nicht vollständig, weil es insgesamt rund 50 solcher Einrichtungen aufzuzählen gibt. Dort scheut man sich längst nicht mehr, auch die für Vorarlberg weniger ruhmreichen Zeiten darzustellen. Dazu kommen private Kunsthäuser und Galerien, Ausstellungsräume von Gemeinden und Firmen, die viel Platz bieten für Kunst von Zeitgenossen aus Vorarlberg und die auch den Austausch fördern.

Shyness Towards Strangers

Anyone who grows up here hears time and again that the typical Voralberger is self-contained and 'Leutscheu' - shy towards and avoiding contact with strangers. Although this sort of Vorarlberger local certainly still exists, the 'Leutscheu' folk are now a distinct minority. You are more likely to meet outgoing and friendly people who will enter into conversation at the drop of a hat. Visitors are often amazed: "When we're out hiking, everyone says hello. I don't even know them, why do they do it?"

The reputation of the Vorarlberg folk for their eccentricity and aloofness is a thing of the past. Anyone who moves to a village in Vorarlberg can expect an invitation to dinner after a few months from one of their neighbours - out of friendliness towards strangers, not for business reasons. There is an affinity for people of the same generation summed up with the local greeting of 'Lieber Jahrgänger'. Some of these 'Jahrgänger' groups (same generation social groups) are highly organised, with regular meetings and events; others limit themselves to one excursion per year or special birthday celebrations. However they are organised though, these groups offer newcomers an opportunity to get to know people of their own age group.

The Cultural Alemanns

The erstwhile perception of the Alemann folk - who don't sing and have no interest in culture, with the exception, perhaps, of Ländler music and military marching music - is also outdated. Today, so many cultural events are held here in all corners of the region that it is impossible for one person to do or see everything. Events include popular highlights such as the Schubertiade (Schubert Festival) in Hohenems and Schwarzenberg, the Bregenz Festival - which even succeeded in attracting James Bond - and a wide range of valuable cultural initiatives from the traditional to the cutting edge.

The Alemann folk like singing and playing music, whether in musical productions, operas, music groups and orchestras. They also enjoy drama, and are full of enthusiasm for farming stories and demanding, intellectual plays. Tradition and culture also comes together at the 123 brass bands in Vorarlberg - an impressive number for the region's 96 communes.

It has been no small achievement for a region on the scale of the Vorarlberg to be able to develop an art gallery like the Kunsthaus at Bregenz harbour. The local history museums - the 'Heimatmuseums' have also been spruced up. Whether the Frauenmuseum (Women's Museum) in Hittisau, the Hohenems Jewish Museum, the Textiles Printing Museum of Hard, the Rhein-Schauen in Lustenau, the Silbertal Mining Museum, the 'Walsermuseum' in Riezlern/ the Little Walser Valley - the list is impressive, and just some of around fifty such attractions that the region boasts. And the museums don't stop short of presenting the less glorious episodes in the history of Vorarlberg either.

„Unsere Freizeit für Ihre Sicherheit" – nach diesem Grundsatz stehen die Frauen und Männer der freiwilligen Feuerwehren im Land bereit. Ein Großereignis ist das jährliche Landesfeuerwehrfest, bei dem zahlreiche Wettkampfgruppen im simulierten Löschangriff gegeneinander antreten. Die durch das Training erworbene Übung wirkt sich natürlich auch bei einem Einsatz im Ernstfall positiv aus.

"Our leisure time for your safety" - it's according to this motto that the men and women of the voluntary fire brigade are ready to assist. One big event: the annual state fire brigade festival in which several groups do competitive battle in a simulated fire fighting mission. The practice gained during training is naturally beneficial in the event of real cases.

Viele der Anlässe im Jahreskreis haben zu tun mit Glaube und Religion. Glauben, vorwiegend römisch-katholischen, gibt es hierzulande noch in allen Spielarten, von traditionell-fundamentalistisch bis fröhlich-aufgeschlossen. Da lassen sich noch Fronleichnamsprozessionen in Prachtentfaltung bewundern, begleitet von Schützenkompanien, oder schlichte Bittprozessionen entlang der Felder.
Markante Zeichen dieser christlich geprägten Kultur sind die Türme der Pfarrkirchen in jeder Gemeinde und Pfarrei, die Kapellen und Bildstöcke an den Straßen. Wir finden auch zahlreiche Klöster im Land, und wenn auch die Zahl der Pfarrer ebenso schrumpft wie jene der Kirchgänger: Wenn neue, nicht christliche religiöse Gruppen Wünsche äußern, dann reagieren nicht wenige Vorarlberger erzkatholisch.

Ein herausragendes Beispiel der Verbindung von Klosterleben und Kultur ist die Propstei St. Gerold im Großen Walsertal. Dort wirkt Propst Nathanael Wirth. Seiner Initiative verdanken Propstei und Tal über die Seelsorge hinaus Jazzseminare und Konzerte, Lesungen und Ausstellungen. Die Angebote zu Seminaren und Meditation werden geschätzt und genutzt und selbstverständlich auch die Speisen und Getränke im Klosterkeller während der warmen Jahreszeit. In der Landwirtschaft, die zur Propstei gehört, floriert seit Jahren die Zucht der bergerprobten Haflingerpferde, deren bedächtige Art sich bewährt beim heilpädagogischen Reiten. Kinder und Erwachsene wissen die Wohltat dieser Therapie zu schätzen, und wenn halt gar kein Geld vorhanden ist, weiß Pater Nathanael Hilfe über den Freundeskreis des kleinen Klosters zu organisieren. Wem auf dem Rücken der Pferde in St. Gerold geholfen wird, der bekommt gewiss ein völlig neues Verständnis für das Motto von Propst Nathanael: „Die Ehre Gottes ist der aufrechte Mensch."

Fasnacht und Feuer

Der Fasching, die alemannische Fasnacht, wird in Vorarlberg mit großen Umzügen und vielen Bällen begangen. Eigene Zünfte sind am Werk und auch manche Einflüsse des rheinischen Karnevals haben den Ursprung nicht völlig überdecken können. Zumindest aus dem Raum Bludenz ist die Fasnacht seit über 750 Jahren bekannt.
Beeindruckend ist allemal das Ende dieses närrischen Treibens, wenn am Funkensonntag nach dem Aschermittwoch in allen Gemeinden des Landes mächtige Holzstöße aufgebaut werden, die abends in Flammen aufgehen. Dieses Funkenabbrennen hat offenbar auch heidnische Wurzeln in den Opferfeuern, mit denen der Winter jeweils endgültig aus dem Land vertrieben werden sollte. Die mit einem Knallkörper gestopfte Hexe, die an der Spitze des Funkens pflichtschuldig explodieren muss, symbolisiert diesen Winter.

Ihren Anteil am kulturellen Leben im Land leisten selbstverständlich auch die zahlreichen Zuwanderergruppen. Das sind die erwähnten Walser; eine starke Gruppe kam dann gegen Ende des 19. Jahrhunderts aus dem Trentin, dem „Welschtirol". Die Südtiroler schließlich wurden unter der Diktatur von Mussolini dazu gezwungen, sich entweder für die italienische Spra-

In addition to the museums there are also private art collections and galleries and exhibition spaces run by local companies and communes, which offer considerable exhibition space for contemporary artists in Vorarlberg and facilitate the buying and selling of art.

Many of the occasions in the regional calendar are connected to faith and religion. The region is predominantly Roman Catholic, with all faiths being represented, from traditional and fundamentalist to charismatic and outgoing. The Corpus Christi processions are a magnificent display, accompanied by rifle companies or Rogation processions across the local fields.
A further striking characteristic of this region's Christian traditions are the towers of the parish churches in every commune and parish, and the roadside chapels and shrines. The region is also home to many monasteries, and even if the number of parish priests and church goers is in decline, whenever new and non-Christian groups express their beliefs, many Vorarlberg folk can be sure to respond with their traditional Catholic views.

The St. Gerold canonry in the Great Walser Valley is an impressive example of the connection between monastery life and culture. Provost Nathanael Wirth works in this area, and the canonry and valley benefit from his initiatives that reach beyond pastoral care to include jazz seminars, concerts, readings and exhibitions. The seminars on offer and meditation classes are valued and used, naturally in addition to the meals and refreshments offered in the monastery crypt. For many years, the breeding of mountain Haflinger horses has also formed part of the farming work of the canonry, whose slow but steady nature has proven itself with therapeutic riding. Children and adults value the benefits of this therapy and when the money isn't there, Peter Nathanael will try and organise some help via the small monastery's circle of acquaintances. Anyone who is helped onto the back of a horse in St. Gerold gains a completely new appreciation for the motto of provost Nathanael: "The honour of God is the upright person."

Carnival and Fire

In Vorarlberg, the festival of Fasching, the Alemannic carnival (Fasnacht), is celebrated with processions and ballroom dances. Different guilds participate and the influences of the Rhineland carnival are yet to have completely blotted out the origin. The Carnival in the Bludenz region looks back on a tradition lasting more than 750 years.
The end of this quixotic tradition is also impressive. On Spark Sunday, which follows Ash Wednesday, large bonfires are built in all corners of the region, which are then lit on the Sunday evening. The burning of the bonfires obviously has its roots in heathen customs, when sacrificial fires were lit to drive the winter out of the land. The winter is symbolised when the stuffed witch that has been tied to the top of the bonfire, and which contains a firecracker, explodes.
It goes without saying that the many immigrant communities also make a big contribution to cultural life in the region. These are the previously mentioned Walser; a large group then arrived towards the end of the 19th

Wer wirklich verwöhnt werden will, ist in einem der vielen hervorragenden Restaurants in Vorarlberg bestens aufgehoben. Hier zaubert der Koch im Landgasthof „Schiffle" in Hohenems gekonnt eine Spezialität des Hauses. Gepflegte Esskultur ist ein wesentlicher Bestandteil Vorarlberger Lebensart.

Those who feel like spoiling themselves are in the best of hands at one of the many excellent restaurants in Vorarlberg. Here, the chef at the country guest house 'Schiffle' puts his professional expertise into action, making a house speciality. Sophisticated cuisine is a key part of the Vorarlberg way of life.

che zu entscheiden oder für das Auswandern. Während des Krieges übersiedelten viele von ihnen auch nach Vorarlberg. Die damals rasch errichteten Südtirolersiedlungen zeugen noch heute von diesem Drama, dem natürlich auch das damals hier herrschende faschistische Regime zugestimmt hatte.
Wenige Jahrzehnte nach Kriegsende herrschte in der aufblühenden Vorarlberger Textilindustrie akuter Mangel an Arbeitskräften. So wurden Zuwanderer aus anderen Bundesländern angeworben, deren Landsmannschaften noch heute stolz auf die Traditionen verweisen. Später wirbt man dann Gastarbeiter aus dem früheren Jugoslawien und schließlich aus der Türkei. Inzwischen wohnen aber zur Wintersaison bereits mehr deutsche Staatsbürger in Vorarlberg als solche mit türkischer Staatsbürgerschaft, weil auch der Zuzug aus der EU eindrucksvoll ist.

Schnapsbrennen

Wer sich wundert, wenn vor ihm auf der Straße ein undefinierbares Gefährt unterwegs ist, gezogen von einem Traktor und bestückt mit einem Kaminabzugsrohr, dem sei ein weiteres Glanzstück an Vorarlberger Brauchtum und wohl auch Kultur ans Herz gelegt, das Schnapsbrennen. Der „Oagabrinnte", der selbstgebrannte Schnaps also, kommt auf den Tisch, wenn abends wohlgelittene Gäste kommen. Weniger willkommenen Leuten wird schon einmal der „Schießhüslar" serviert, der völlig misslungen ist.

Als letztes Bundesland Österreichs kennt Vorarlberg noch die fahrbare Schnapsbrennerei. An die 100 solcher Destillen werden von Genossenschaften oder Obst- und Gartenbauvereinen betrieben und gegen Entgelt an die über 2.000 Brennberechtigten im Land verliehen. Wer selbst Obst besitzt oder Beeren, darf 100 l reinen Alkohol brennen, also bei 42 % Alkohol knapp 240 l Schnaps. Meist kommen Birne und Apfel in den Brennhafen, aber auch Zwetschke, Kirsche, Marille, Quitte und Beeren ergeben spezielle klare Wässerchen. Gefragt sind dabei sortenreine Brände, deshalb finden sich gerade unter den Selbstgebrannten in Vorarlberg zahlreiche Spezialitäten. Und für einzelne alte Bauernhöfe gilt sogar noch das Privileg nach Maria Theresia; diese Bauern dürfen deshalb 300 l Alkohol brennen – also 720 l steuerbegünstigten Schnaps. Nachvollziehbar ist zudem, dass bei solchen Voraussetzungen auch die VAKÖ, die „Vereinigung der Abfindungs- und Kleinbrenner Österreichs" ihren Sitz in Vorarlberg hat, inklusive Vereinsleitung.

Selbstverständlich sind auch zahlreiche andere Vereine im Land aktiv, ob in Sachen Sport, Geselligkeit, Kultur, soziales Engagement oder Katastrophenhilfe, Umwelt- und Naturschutz, religiöse Dienste oder Nachbarschaftshilfe – die meisten Vorarlberger engagieren sich in mindestens einem Verein. 6.468 Frauen und Männer stehen im Land etwa bereit, wenn es gilt, zu einem Schadenfeuer, einem Unfalleinsatz oder einem technischen Einsatz auszurücken. 120 freiwillige Ortsfeuerwehren und ebenso freiwillig organisierte Wehren in 27 größeren Betrieben leisten Großartiges.
Dass sie zudem zu feiern verstehen, beweisen die Feuerwehren, Musikkapellen und viele weitere Vereine immer wieder. Zu den Festen, die fixer Bestandteil sind im Jahresablauf, sind alle herzlich eingeladen. Feiern wir also mit!

century from Trentin, the 'Welsch Tyrol'. During the Mussolini dictatorship, the South Tyrolean folk in Italy were forced either to speak Italian or leave the country. During the war, many of these people came to Vorarlberg and the rapidly established south Tyrolean communities - welcomed by the fascist regime then in power here - pay testimony to this drama to this day.

In the decades after the end of the war, the then booming textiles industry in Vorarlberg suffered from an acute shortage of labour. The first new arrivals came from the other federal regions of Austria, whose traditions are proudly maintained by their homeland associations today. Later, guest workers were invited from the former Yugoslavia, and subsequently Turkey. During the winter season, more German citizens now live in Vorarlberg than those of Turkish origin, with immigration from within the EU also being significant here.

Schnapps Distilling

Anyone who beholds an indefinable contraption on the road being pulled along by a tractor and equipped with a chimney pipe, is likely to be beholding another gem of Vorarlberg traditions and culture - schnapps distilling. 'Oagabrinnte', or self-distilled schnapps, goes onto the table when well-liked guests are present. Less welcome guests are served with 'Schießhüslar', the unsuccessful vintages.

As the last remaining federal region of Austria to do so, Vorarlberg also offers mobile schnapps distilling, with 100 such distilleries being operated by fruit growing and horticultural associations, and also provided to the region's more than 2,000 registered distillers. Anyone who has fruit or berries themselves is able to distil 100 l of pure alcohol, which works out at almost 240 l of schnapps with 42 % alcohol. Apples and pears are mostly distilled, although damsons, cherries, apricots, quince and berries also result in particularly clear vintages. Authentic flavours are especially popular, which means there are a wide range of specialities among the distilleries in Vorarlberg. And the 'Maria Theresia' privilege also applies to certain old farms, which are accordingly permitted to distil 300 l of alcohol - or 720 l of tax-deductible schnapps.

It is understandable, therefore, that the VÄKO organisation - The Association of Austrian Home Distillers - is also based in Vorarlberg, including its management.

Many other associations are also active in the region, whether in the area of sports, recreation, culture, social causes and emergency aid, environmental and nature protection, religious services or neighbourly help – and most Vorarlbergers are members of at least one association.
6,468 men and women are on call in the event of a fire, an accident or a technical call-out. The 120 voluntary local fire brigades, and voluntary fire brigades in 27 large organisations do a great job.
The fire brigades, music associations, and wide range of other associations certainly know how to put on a good celebration. Everyone is welcome to the parties and celebrations which are a regular fixture in the local events calendar. So let's join in and have a great time!

Sommer auf dem Bodensee. Wie Edelsteine glitzern die Sonnenstrahlen auf den Wellen und die Hohentwiel, der letzte Raddampfer auf dem See, zieht ihre Bahn. Das von der Königlich Württembergischen Dampfschifffahrt (KWD) in Auftrag gegebene Schiff lief 1913 vom Stapel. Nach wechselvoller Geschichte sollte es 1984 eigentlich verschrottet werden und konnte nur dank Privatinitiative gerettet und mit großem Aufwand nach Originalplänen wieder instand gesetzt werden. Jetzt schafft die 950 PS starke 2-Zylinder-Dampfmaschine wieder 16,7 Knoten (31 km/h).

Summer at Lake Constance. The sunlight shimmers over the waves like gemstones and the Hohentwiel, the last paddle steamer on the lake, ploughs through the waters. This vessel, commissioned by the 'Königlich Württembergische Dampfschifffahrt' (KWD) was first launched in 1913. After a rich history, it was originally to have been scrapped in 1984, but was saved thanks to a private initiative, refurbished according to its original design and made seaworthy once more at great cost. The 950 HP, 2 cylinder steam engine now has a top speed of 16,7 knots (31 km/h).

Zur Gasthauskultur in Vorarlberg gehören keineswegs nur Speiserestaurants, es gibt auch noch die alten Dorfwirtshäuser. Die heißen besonders im Bregenzerwald nicht selten „Zum Ochsen“, wie das Schild aus Egg zeigt, oder der Blick in den „Ochsen“ von Schwarzenberg, natürlich gibt es auch den singenden Ochsenwirt in Sulzberg, den Ochsen in Hittisau oder in Alberschwende – lauter Hinweise auf die Gespanne, deren Fuhrleute einst wohl gern zugekehrt sind.

The hospitality culture in Vorarlberg doesn't simply include restaurants, there are also many traditional village inns and taverns. In the Bregenz Forest, these are often called 'Zum Ochsen'(the ox), as shown on the sign from Egg, or the view into the 'Ochsen' at Schwarzenberg, there's naturally also the 'singender Ochsenwirt' in Sulzberg, and 'den Ochsen' in Hittisau or in Alberschwende - reminders of the harnessed teams, the drivers of whom enjoyed staying in these inns in times gone by.

In den Gebirgstälern Vorarlbergs reicht der Schutzwald oft nicht aus, um Siedlungsgebiete oder Verkehrsverbindungen vor Lawinen zu bewahren. Damit das Leben auch in schneereichen Wintern möglichst sicher bleibt, sind an manchen Hängen massive Verbauungen erforderlich. Sie bieten Dörfern wie Lech Schutz.

In the mountain valleys of Vorarlberg, protective forest coverage is often insufficient to protect settlements or transport routes from avalanches. To make sure that life during the snowy winters here is as safe as possible, massive control structures are necessary on some hillsides. They offer protection to villages such as Lech.

Ein Höhepunkt der Brauchtumspflege in Vorarlberg ist der Funkensonntag, also der Sonntag nach Aschermittwoch. Da lodern im ganzen Land die Funken. Historiker debattieren, ob hier ein uralter heidnischer Brauch überlebt habe oder ob mit dem Abbrennen des Funkens das Ende des Faschings im schwäbisch-alemannischen Kulturraum begangen wird. Während in manchen Gemeinden des Landes der Funkensonntag zum „Event" gewandelt wurde, geht es in der Gemeinde St. Gerold im Großen Walsertal tatsächlich noch um den Funken. Früher schlichteten Vereine und Kinder den Funken auf, seit zehn Jahren nimmt sich eine eigene Funkenzunft des Brauches an. Ein Erfolg ist der Abend, wenn die Hexe als Sinnbild des Winters mit lautem Knall explodiert. Andere Funkenzünfte im Land binden aus Gründen der Ausgeglichenheit seit einigen Jahren ein Hexenpaar auf den Funken ...

A highlight of the local traditions in Vorarlberg is 'spark Sunday', the Sunday after Ash Wednesday. This event sees the burning of bonfires across the whole state. Historians argue as to whether this is the survival or an ancient heathen custom, or the burning of the bonfires was to celebrate the end of the Fasching carnival in Swabian-Alemmanic culture. Whilst in some of the state's communes, Spark Sunday has become an 'event', in the commune of St. Gerold in the Great Walser Valley, it is the bonfires themselves which are the event. In times gone by, youth clubs and children would build the bonfires. For the last ten years, this has been the task of a bonfire guild. The evening is considered a success if the witch, who is a symbol for winter, explodes with a loud bang. For reasons of harmony, other bonfire guilds tie a pair of witches to the bonfire ...

Ein Kirchenmann als Pferdeflüsterer: Das Unsichtbare hinter dem Sichtbaren erahnen zu lassen, das ist ein Angebot der Propstei St. Gerold im Großen Walsertal, als deren Gründungsjahr 960 gilt. Zu den irdischen und himmlischen Angeboten, die Propst Nathanael Wirth und sein Team offerieren, gehört das heilpädagogische Reiten. Die dem Schweizer Benediktinerkloster Einsiedeln zugeordnete Niederlassung ist dem Pater aus der Schweiz seit 1958 Heimat. Dass er seinen Militärdienst bei der Schweizer Armee einst als Kavallerist geleistet hat, kommt ihm beim Umgang mit den Pferden gewiss zugute.

A churchman as a horse whisperer: Being able to perceive the unseen behind the visible is an offer of Provost's residence St. Gerold in the Great Walser Valley dating from the year of its foundation, 960. The earthly and heavenly services that Provost Nathanael Wirth and his team offer include therapeutic horse riding. This branch, allotted to the hermitage of the Swiss Benedictine cloister, has been the home to the Father from Switzerland since 1958. Having completed his military service in the cavalry of the Swiss army, he certainly knows a thing or two about horses.

„Tracht ist ein anderes Wort für Vielfalt", meint Dr. Paul Rachbauer, Obmann des Vorarlberger Landestrachtenverbandes. Diese Aufnahmen aus Sonntag im Großen Walsertal vermitteln einen Eindruck davon. Zur erneuerten Frauentracht gehört seit 50 Jahren der schwarze Hut, die kleine Miriam trägt das filigrane Schäppili der Mädchen.

"Costume is another word for diversity" says Dr. Paul Rachbauer, representative of the Vorarlberg state costume association. These images from Sonntag in the Great Walser Valley provide an impression of this. Black hats have been part of the traditional women's costume for 50 years. Little Miriam is wearing the felt 'Schäppili' worn by girls.

Zugegeben, die beiden Frauen sind einander in der Oberstadt von Bregenz nicht ganz zufällig begegnet. Umso überraschter ist der Fotograf, als Betül Akten, in Vorarlberg geborene Muslima türkischer Abstammung, und Sr. Joanita vom Kloster Marienberg einander als alte Bekannte begrüßen: Man kennt einander von kurzen Besuchen der Vorarlbergerin bei einer Freundin in der Klosterschule des Klosters und von Seminaren der angehenden Kinderbetreuerin.

Granted, these two women didn't meet each other in the upper town of Bregenz coincidentally. The photographer is surprised, however, as Betül Akten, a Muslim of Turkish extraction born in Vorarlberg, and Sister Joanita of Marienberg convent greet each other as old friends: they know each other from the brief visits made by Mrs. Aktem to a friend at the convent school in the convent and from seminars attended by the budding child carer.

Landschaft, Kultur und Architektur am Bodensee: Der Hafen der Landeshauptstadt Bregenz mit dem Vorarlberger Landesmuseum, dem Theater am Kornmarkt und dem Kunsthaus Bregenz, darüber die neugotische Pfarrkirche Herz Jesu und direkt am Hafen das Postamt aus Zeit der k. k. Monarchie in Ringstraßen-Architektur. Rechts das erste in Vorarlberg errichtete Badezimmer, das mit fließendem Warm- und Kaltwasser ausgestattet war. Es findet sich in der Villa Raczinsky, 1875 bis 1881 oberhalb von Bregenz vom polnischen Grafen Carl Eduard Natecz v. Raczinsky für seine Frau Caroline Therese, geb. Prinzessin Öttingen-Wallerstein, erbaut. Nach dem Tod seiner geliebten Gattin verließ der Graf Bregenz, 1904 übernahm der Orden der Dominikanerinnen das Anwesen. Heute sind dort Gäste willkommen, in der prachtvoll renovierten Villa finden Tagungen und Seminare statt.

Scenery, culture and architecture at Lake Constance: The harbour of the state capital, Bregenz, with the Vorarlberg Landesmuseum, the theatre on the Kornmarkt and the Bregenz Kunsthaus (art gallery). Above: the neogothic parish church ‚Herz Jesu' and right on the harbour the post office which dates from the era of the imperial and royal monarchy and was built in the 'Ringstraßen' architectural style. Right: the first bathroom that was built in Vorarlberg to offer running hot and cold water. It is located in the Villa Raczinsky, built from 1875 to 1881 above Bregenz by the Polish count Carl Eduard Natecz v. Raczinsky for his wife Mrs. Caroline Therese, born the Princess of Öttingen-Wallerstein. After the death of his beloved wife, the count left Bregenz. In 1904, the Dominican order took over the property. Today, the splendidly renovated villa welcomes visitors as a location of conferences and seminars.

Architektur im Alpenraum hat nicht zwangsläufig Heustädel im Format XXL zur Folge. Das Silvretta-Haus auf der Bielerhöhe, auf 2.040 m Seehöhe über dem Silvrettastausee, spricht die Sprache der vorgegebenen Landschaft ebenso wie der Technik. So zeichnet die Frontfassade den Schwung der Staumauer nach. Die Nutzung der Sonne für die Energiegewinnung entspricht der Philosophie des Eigentümers, der Vorarlberger Illwerke AG.
Wehrhafte Architektur aus dem 14. und 15. Jahrhundert im Bild rechts: Die Burg Neu-Ems oder Schloss Glopper oberhalb der Stadt Hohenems entstand 1343 und wurde nach der Zerstörung im Appenzellerkrieg 1408 erneut aufgebaut. Die spätgotische Anlage wird von der Besitzerfamilie bewohnt.

Architecture in the alpine region isn't just about the construction of super-sized hay barns. The Silvretta Haus on the Bielerhöhe pass, overlooking the man-made Silvretta lake at 2,040 meters above sea level, speaks the language of both its surroundings and technology. Its front facade, for instance, traces the curves of the dam. Its use of solar energy corresponds with the philosophy of the owners, Vorarlberger Illwerke AG.
Well-fortified architecture from the 14th and 15th centuries: Neu-Ems castle (also known as Glopper castle) above the town of Hohenems was originally built in 1343, before being destroyed in the Appenzell war and then being rebuilt in 1408. The late gothic edifice is still inhabited by the owning family.

Wer in einer Gemeinde im Bregenzerwald nach dem Pfarrhof Ausschau hält, wird oft ein Haus finden, das diesem Beispiel ziemlich ähnlich sieht. Der Pfarrhof von Schoppernau, 1806 errichtet und liebevoll restauriert, ist ein markantes Beispiel für ein „Widum", wie das Wohnhaus des Ortspfarrers auch genannt worden ist. Der moderne Bau rechts, ein großes Privatobjekt, greift heimische Traditionen auf, ohne sie nur zu kopieren.

Schoppernau bietet auch weitere Beispiele aktueller Vorarlberger Holzbauarchitektur. Im Bild oben das Gerätehaus der Feuerwehr und dahinter das Mehrzweckgebäude von Schoppernau mit Tourismusbüro oder dem Franz-Michel-Felder-Museum. Darüber nochmals der Pfarrhof.

Those who look for the parsonage in any commune in the Bregenz Forest will often stumble across a house which is similar to this example. Schoppernau parsonage, built in 1806 and lovingly restored, is a prime example of a 'Widum', as the residence of the parish priest is also known. The modern building on the right, a large privately owned property, takes its inspiration from local traditions, without simply copying them.

Shoppernau also provides further examples of contemporary timber constructed architecture in Vorarlberg, such as the garage for the fire brigade, and behind it, the Schoppernau district centre with the tourist office and the Franz-Michel-Felder Museum. Above: another impression of the Parsonage.

Einen herausragenden Ruf haben sich während der vergangenen Jahre die Bregenzer Festspiele erworben. Die Seeaufführungen und die Produktionen im Haus finden international großes Echo. Die Bregenzer Seebühne gilt mit ihren 7.000 Sitzplätzen als größte Freilicht-Festspielbühne der Welt, das Abenteuer begann 1946 mit einer Bühne, die auf zwei vor dem Ufer vertäuten Kiesschiffen gebaut wurde, als „Bregenzer Festwoche". Die Seebühne und besonders das Festspiel- und Kongresshaus (eröffnet 1979, erweitert 2006) ermöglichen ein abwechslungsreiches Programm. Die Architektur des Hauses weiß zu beeindrucken, markant die „Ready Maid", geschaffen von Gottfried Bechtold.
Oben das Bühnenbild für Giacomo Puccinis „Tosca", aufgeführt 2007 und 2008. Das Auge beeindruckte die Filmcrew der James-Bond-Serie so sehr, dass sie im Frühjahr 2008 eine längere Sequenz der Agentenoper „Quantum of Solace" in Bregenz drehte.

In recent years, the Bregenz Festspiele (festival) has gained an outstanding reputation, with both the lakeside and indoor productions finding widespread international praise. With its 7,000 seats, the Bregenz lakeside stage is the biggest open air theatrical stage in the world. The adventure started in 1946 as the 'Bregenz Festwoche', with a stage that was built on two gravel ships moored before the river banks. The lakeside stage, and particularly the Festival House (opened 1979, extended 2006) facilitate a particularly varied programme. The architecture of the House is impressive, especially the sculpture 'Ready Maid', created by Gottfried Bechtold.
Above: the stage setting for Giacamo Puccini's 'Tosca', performed in 2007 and 2008. The film crew of the James Bond series was so much impressed by the eye that they shot a long scene of the agent story "Quantum of Solace" in Bregenz in spring.

Hohenems markiert den Start einer Erfolgsgeschichte, die 1976 mit den ersten Konzerten der Schubertiade begann. Diese gilt längst als das bedeutendste Schubertfestival. Im gekonnt zum Konzertsaal umgebauten Markus-Sittikus-Saal finden seit 2005 herausragende Konzerte statt, ein weiterer gefragter Veranstaltungsort der Schubertiade ist Schwarzenberg. Im Mittelpunkt stehen die Werke des Komponisten Franz Schubert (1797 - 1828).

Hohenems celebrates the start of a success story which began with the first concerts of the 'Schubertiade' in 1976, and has now been the world's leading Schubert festival for some years. Since 2005, top notch concerts have been held at the Markus-Sittikus Hall which has been skilfully renovated into a concert hall. Schwarzenberg is another venue for the Schubertiade. The festival predominantly draws on the works of composer Franz Schubert (1797 - 1828).

Vor dem endgültigen Zerfall gerettet hat die Familie Spiegel das ca. 300 Jahre alte Rheintalhaus im Zentrum von Haselstauden. Keller und Fundament sind noch etwas älter, aus der Zeit des Dreißigjährigen Krieges, also der ersten Hälfte des 17. Jahrhunderts. Verschiedene Zimmermannszeichen an Balken verweisen darauf, dass das Haus einmal versetzt, also wohl am Haselstauder Berg abgebrochen und am heutigen Standort neu aufgebaut wurde. Als Otto und Laurel Spiegel das Haus 1985 von der Stadt Dornbirn erwarben, waren vom Keller aus die Sterne zu sehen. Immer wieder neu zeigt sich Otto Spiegel von der „Klimaanlage" des Rheintalhauses begeistert, die mit einfachsten Mitteln auskommt. Die vorragenden „Klebedächer" über den Fenstern sorgen im Hochsommer für Schatten, wenn die Sonne im Winter tief steht, bringen die gewölbten Untersichten hingegen zusätzlich Licht und Wärme in die Räume. Große Rheintalhäuser, wie das Spiegelhaus, sind in Vorarlberg etwa ab 1700 nachgewiesen, zuvor wurde eine kleinere, niedrigere Ausgabe gebaut. „Obwohl die Arbeit an einem solch alten Haus nie ausgeht, könnten wir nie mehr umziehen!", zeigt sich Otto Spiegel überzeugt, den eigentlich seine aus den USA stammende Frau mit ihrer Liebe zu alten Häusern angesteckt hatte.

The Spiegel family saved the ca. 300 years old Rheintalhaus in the centre of Haselstauden from ruin. Its cellars and foundations are somewhat older, dating from the time of the thirty years war, in the first half of the 17th century. The differing carpenters' signatures on the timber point to the house having been first constructed at Haselstauder Berg before being dismantled and rebuilt at its present location. When Otto and Laurel Spiegel bought the house from the town of Dornbirn in 1985, the cellar was open to the skies. Otto Spiegel is continually enthused about the 'climate control system' of the Rheintalhaus which runs at an exceptionally cheap rate. The special covers which project over the windows provide shade during the summer and thanks to their concave design, bring light and heat into the room when the sun is low in the skies during the winter. Large Rhine valley houses like the Spiegelhaus were first built in Vorarlberg subsequent to 1700. Before this, such houses were smaller and lower constructions. "Although the work on an old house like this never lets up, we could never move!" says Otto Spiegel, whose wife, originally from the USA, infected him with her love for old houses.

Die Kultur des Bauens in Vorarlberg hat ab etwa 1980 eine erstaunliche Entwicklung genommen. Aus diesem kleinen Land gab es eine Reihe von Anstößen, die weite Kreise gezogen haben und heute an Architektur interessierte Besucher ins Land bringen. Einer der Architekten, die im Land und darüber hinaus einen hervorragenden Ruf genießen, ist Arno Bereiter, Lustenau. Das von ihm entworfene Wohnhaus in Lustenau zeugt von der oft radikalen Abkehr von Siedlungshäusern mit Satteldach und Kniestock, mit bewussten Rückgriffen auf heimisches Baumaterial und bewährte Formen. Schlafräume mit Nasszellen finden sich im „Turm", der in etwa die gleiche Höhe aufweist, wie die Giebelhöhe eines großen Rheintalhauses. Flexibel der ebenerdige Wohnbereich, selbst die Küche lässt sich umstellen. Drei verschieden ausgerichtete, überdachte Sitzterrassen lassen den Bewohnern die Auswahl. Und die vorragenden Dächer sorgen bei Sommerhitze für Schatten und stehen der Wintersonne nicht im Weg.

Since 1980, the culture of building in Vorarlberg has completed an astounding development. From this small region outwards, there have been a series of impulses which have created a stir and attracted visitors interested in architecture to the region. One of the architects who enjoys a name both here and beyond is Arno Bereiter from Lustenau. The Wohnhaus (residence) designed by him in Lustenau attests to the often radical break from residential housing with gabled roofs and flap tiles, with conscious recourse to local construction materials and proven designs. The 'tower' contains bedrooms with en suite bathrooms, and is about the same height as the gable height of a large Rhine valley house. The ground-level living area is flexible and even the kitchen can be moved. Residents are able to choose between three differently designed, covered patios. The projecting roofs provide shade on hot summer's days but do not block out the winter sunlight.

Seit 1688 steht dieser Bauernhof in Lech, Ortsteil Stubenbach, eines der eindrucksvollen Beispiele für nachhaltige Architektur in einer anscheinend unzugänglichen Landschaft. Im Winter gab es einst für die Bewohner von hier oft wochenlang kein Wegkommen, wenn der Schnee sich meterhoch türmte. Inzwischen wird der längst verlassen gewesene Hof als Feriendomizil genutzt und möglichst original erhalten, wie der neu gebaute und traditionell aus Holz „gestrickte" Stadel zeigt.

Eines der zahlreichen Zeichen der Volksfrömmigkeit im Land ist das geschnitzte Wegkreuz an der Strecke von Bizau Richtung Hirschberg, unweit des Berghauses Kanisfluh.

This farmhouse in Lech in the district of Stubenbach has been standing since 1688 and is one of the most impressive examples of lasting architecture in apparently inaccessible countryside. In earlier times, with the snow several meters high, local residents would often find themselves isolated for weeks on end. The farmhouse, which was left abandoned for many years, is now used as a holiday home and has been renovated in a style which has ensured the preservation of the building's original features, such as the newly constructed wooden barn.

One of the many signs of popular piety in the region: a carved roadside cross on the road from Bizau to Hirschberg not far from the 'Berghaus Kanisfluh' hotel.

Der Widderstein in den Allgäuer Alpen, die höchste Erhebung im Kleinwalsertal, ist ein beliebtes Kletterziel.

The Widderstein in the Allgau Alps, the highest elevation in the Little Walser Valley, is a popular climbing destination.

Die Vielfalt einer Kulturlandschaft The Diversity of a Cultural Landscape

LANDSCHAFT VORARLBERG THE VORARLBERG LANDSCAPE

Markanter Fels im Dachgeschoss des Landes: Den Talabschluss im Montafon markiert wuchtig der Piz Buin, Vorarlbergs höchster Berg (3.312 m), hier vom Hohen Rad aus aufgenommen. Die Platten im Vordergrund sind Silvretta-Gneis. Wie viele der Berge und Orte in diesem Landesteil trägt auch der Piz Buin einen rätoromanischen Namen. Übersetzt würde er schlicht „Ochsenspitze" heißen. Da bleiben die Vorarlberger doch lieber bei der rätoromanischen Bezeichnung …

Prominent rock formations in the region's uppermost storey: the close of the valley in Montafon is marked out by the prominent massif of Piz Buin, the highest mountain in Vorarlberg (3,312 m), viewed here from the perspective of Hohen Rad. The rocks in the foreground are Silvretta-Gneis. Like many of the mountains and places in this part of the region, the Piz Buin also has a Rhaeto-Romanic name. Translated, the name would be "Oxen Peak". The local residents doubtlessly prefer the Rhaeto-Romanic version …

Von „Restösterreich", wie die Vorarlberger die Alpenrepublik außerhalb ihres Bundeslandes gern nennen, ist der westlichste Teil durch massive Felsformationen getrennt. Über die Jahrhunderte blieb dieser Felsriegel schwer zu überwinden, er barg dem Reisenden manche Gefahr. Als im Oktober 1414 einer der drei damals konkurrierenden Päpste, Johannes XXIII., zum Konzil nach Konstanz reiste, nahm er den Weg über den Arlberg. Dass sein Fuhrwerk auf der Passhöhe umkippte und der Papst im Schnee landete, darf als schlechtes Vorzeichen gedeutet werden. Wenig später setzte ihn das Konzil ab, weshalb 1958 Angelo Giuseppe Roncalli nach seiner Wahl zum Papst ebenfalls den Namen Johannes XXIII. annehmen konnte.
Trotz all dieser Reiseprobleme erhoben sich warnende Stimmen, als 1879 der Bau des Eisenbahntunnels durch den Berg begann. „Was Gott durch einen Berg getrennt hat", so meinten manche Vorarlberger, „das soll der Mensch nicht durch ein Loch verbinden!" 1884 war es aber doch so weit und bereits ein Jahr später wurde in dem über 10 km langen Arlbergtunnel das zweite Gleis verlegt, weil die neue Verbindung so gut angenommen wurde.

In diesem Landesteil ragen die Felsriesen bis über 3.000 m empor, hier erstrecken sich die Gletscher. Ob Silvretta, Rätikon oder Verwall – manche der Gipfel und Wände stellen an Kletterer höchste Anforderungen, wollen mit Umsicht bezwungen werden. Daneben finden sich gangbare Wege, die auch dem ambitionierten Wanderer erschlossen bleiben. Der harte Bergwinter, einst gefürchtet, hat sich längst zum Wintertraum gewandelt und Vorarlberg zum begehrten Reiseziel gemacht. Es waren weitblickende Pioniere, die bereits vor über 100 Jahren erkannt haben, welche Möglichkeiten sich an tief verschneiten Hängen auftun. Nicht umsonst sind Arlberg und Montafon, Bregenzerwald und Brandnertal weitum geschätzte Zentren des Wintersportes, ergänzt durch eine Reihe kleiner Wintersportgebiete, wie etwa im Laternsertal oder im Großen Walsertal.
Im Sommer und Herbst sorgen erfahrene Berg- und Wanderführer für sicheren Tritt auf steilem Weg, zur Winterszeit machen in Vorarlberg die Skilehrerinnen und Skilehrer unzählige Neulinge der Pisten vertraut mit dem richtigen Umgang mit Ski und Snowboard. Sie begleiten gern auch Touren in Gebiete, in denen nichts zu hören und zu sehen ist vom Rummel einer Schneebar. Wer den Aufstieg wagt, dem bietet das Winterwunderland Vorarlberg jene Erlebnisse und Eindrücke, von denen Ernest Hemingway ebenso zu schwärmen verstand wie seither zahlreiche mehr und weniger prominente Besucherinnen und Besucher. Ob jemand im Privatberuf eine Königskrone trägt oder seine Fans als Spitzensportler und Leinwandstar begeistert – dick vermummt auf einem Tiefschneehang sind sie alle einfach begeisterte Vorarlberg-Fans. Dass viele zu Stammgästen werden, stellt der Landschaft ein wohl ebenso gutes Zeugnis aus wie all den Menschen, die sich um die Urlauber bemühen.

Lacus Brigantinus – so benannten die Römer einst den Bodensee, zumindest den sogenannten Obersee, nach den keltischen Brigantiern, die vor ihnen Bregenz besiedelt hatten. Den einen ist der See Eingangstor nach Vorarlberg, den anderen das logische Ende, weil in ihn die Gewässer münden, die aus den Gebirgszügen und Talschaften fließen. Lediglich der Lech und die Breitach nehmen einen anderen Weg; ihr Wasser rinnt nicht über den Rhein in

As the local people of Vorarlberg like to call the Alpine Republic beyond their federal region, their western part is separated from the 'rest of Austria' by massive rock formations. Over the centuries, this rock formation proved hard to overcome, presenting travellers with some danger. When, in October 1414, one of the three rival popes of the era, Johannes XXIII travelled to the synod in Konstanz, his route took him over the Arlberg. The fact that his coach overturned on the mountain pass and the pope ended up in the snow was interpreted as being a bad omen. A little later, he was deposed by the synod, which is why Angelo Giuseppe Roncalli was also able to assume the name Johannes XXIII after having been voted pope in 1958.
Despite all of the travel problems, voices of warning were raised when the construction of the railway tunnel through the mountain started. "That which God has separated by a mountain should not be connected with a tunnel by man," was the view of some Vorarlbergers. The railway was completed by 1884 however, and just one year later, the second set of tracks were laid in the Arlberg tunnel, with a total length of more than 10 km, as the new connection had been such a success.

In this part of the region, the giant crags tower over 3,000 m over sea level, and glaciers also span across the rocks. Whether the Silvretta, Rätikon or Verwall - some of the peaks and rock faces provide the toughest challenge to climbers and should be tackled with caution. There are also passable routes which are open to ambitious hikers. The hard mountain winter which was once feared has long since turned into a winter's dream and made Vorarlberg a coveted tourist destination. Forward looking pioneers were able to recognise the possibilities offered by snow covered slopes more than 100 years ago. It isn't for nothing that Arlberg, Montafon, the Bregenz forest and the Brandner Valley are now widely popular centres for winter sports, supplemented by a wide range of smaller winter sports locations such as the Laterns Valley or the Great Walser Valley.
In the summer and autumn, experienced mountaineers and hiking guides ensure safe walking over the steep paths. Every winter in Vorarlberg, skiing instructors teach innumerable newcomers to the slopes the correct way of using a pair of skis or a snowboard. They also accompany tours through isolated areas which are a far cry from the conviviality of a snow bar. For those adventurous enough to ascend, the winter wonderland of Vorarlberg offers those experiences and impressions that were the subject of Ernest Hemingway's enthusiasm and numerous other visitors of greater or lesser fame since then. Whether a visitor wears a royal crown during their working day, or enthuses their fans as a top sportsman or star of the screen, when wrapped up on the snowy slopes they're just another enthusiastic fan of the Vorarlberg. The fact that so many become regular visitors isn't just thanks to the charming landscape and scenery, it is also down to the people who attend to the holiday makers.

Lacus Brigantinus - such was the name given to Lake Constance - at least the so-called 'lake superior' part of the lake - by the Romans, after the Celtic brigands who had colonised Bregenz before them. On the one hand, the lake is an entrance door to Vorarlberg, on the other, its logical ending, since

Viele Gebiete in Vorarlberg bieten sich an zu geruhsamer Erholung ebenso wie zu sportlicher Betätigung. Die Bilder zeigen Mountainbiker am Golm im Montafon und den bekannten Vorarlberger Bergsteiger Beat Kammerlander an den Kirchlispitzen im Rätikon.

Many places in Vorarlberg are ideal for quiet relaxation and sporting activity. These images show mountain bikers at Golm in Montafon, and the well-known Vorarlberg climber Beat Kammerlander on the Kirchlispitzen in Rätikon.

die Nordsee, sondern über die Donau ins Schwarze Meer. Wenn sich nach einem heißen Sommertag die Sonne glutrot zu ihrem abendlichen Bad in den Bodensee begibt, dann wissen die Vorarlberger im Rheintal: Der nächste Tag wird ebenso strahlend schön sein wie der zur Neige gehende. Taucht die Sonne aber in grellem Gelb ins Wasser, so sieht es für den Kundigen nach Regen aus. Gäste bestaunen dieses beeindruckende Wechselspiel der Farben, das am Abend die Felsschrofen und Gipfel, die das Rheintal säumen, ganz unterschiedlich erglühen lässt. Der gewitzte Vorarlberger wird bei entsprechenden Anfragen darauf verweisen, dass es sich dabei um einen Service des Vorarlberg Tourismus für die Urlauber handle, unendlich viel eindrucksvoller als das noch so prachtvollste Feuerwerk.

Der See ist der Rest eines erheblich größeren Gewässers, das sich nach dem Rückzug der Gletscher bis weit nach Graubünden erstreckte, der Talboden lag deutlich unter dem jetzigen Niveau. Über die Jahrtausende füllten der Rhein und die seitlichen Zuflüsse dieses Tal auf. Wie jung im sogenannten Unterland, also in Seenähe, der gewachsene Boden ist, zeigen die Riede und Moorflächen, die meisten von ihnen erst im vergangenen Jahrhundert trocken gelegt. Dort wurde bis vor wenigen Jahrzehnten noch Torf gestochen und als Heizmaterial verwendet. Spuren der Gletscher finden sich als „Gletscherschliff" besonders an Felswänden entlang des Rheintales.

Das alles kann man bedenken, wenn man den überall öffentlich zugänglichen Gestaden des Sees entlangwandert oder -radelt, es reicht aber gewiss auch, in einem der Bäder lediglich die Natur zu genießen, die Segelboote und Fischergondeln auf dem See zu beobachten. Mit der Bodenseeschifffahrt lässt sich der See in alle Richtungen durchpflügen, die Schifffahrtsunternehmen rund um den See wirken dabei zusammen. Bei solchen Lustfahrten lässt sich vom Wasser aus bewundern, was sich mit dem Fahrrad oder bei Wanderungen auch am Ufer erschließt.

Ornithologen zeigen sich begeistert von der Vogelwelt im Rheindelta, das im Jahr 1900 entstand. Damals erst war der Neue Rhein völlig ausgebaggert, der das Wasser des nach Unwettern oft reißenden Flusses auf geradem Weg in den See leitete. So sollten die früher regelmäßigen Überschwemmungen des Tales verhindert werden. Nach wie vor wird am Rhein und seiner Entschärfung gearbeitet, inzwischen mit dem Ziel, ihm wo möglich mehr an Raum zu geben, damit bei Hochwasser nicht gleich die Dammkrone erreicht wird.

Es ist Natur aus zweiter Hand, wie etwa vor der Marktgemeinde Hard, die ihr Prädikat „am Bodensee" zu verlieren drohte, weil der Neue Rhein mit seinen gewaltigen Mengen an Schwemmmaterial die einst 50 m tiefe Bucht innert 50 Jahren vollständig auflandete. Die Bucht wurde ausgebaggert und mit einem Damm geschützt, entlang der weit in den See vorgezogenen Rheinmündung bildeten sich Biotope, sanft unterstützt durch Flussbaufachleute und Naturschützer. Das gilt auch vor dem Rheindelta, nur bildet dort der Polderdamm einen markanten Abschluss.

this is also where the waters flow from the mountain ranges and mountain valleys. It is only the Lech and the Breitach which take another route; their water does not flow to the North Sea via the Rhine, but via the Danube to the Black Sea. When the sun glows red at the end of a warm summer's day and sets into Lake Constance, then the Vorarlberg folks in the Rhine valley know one thing: the next day will be equally as beautiful as the one which has just come to an end. If the sun sets into the waters in a bright yellow, however, then those in the know will predict rain. Visitors enjoy this impressive interplay of colours which gives the rocky crags and peaks which surround the Rhine valley their different glow. With the corresponding enquiry, the shrewd Vorarlberger will point out that this is an additional service from the Vorarlberg tourism to holidaymakers, much more impressive than the most splendid fireworks display.

The lake itself is the remnants of a large body of water which after the retreat of the glaciers stretched all the way to Graubünden, and the valley floor was clearly beneath the current level of the lake. Over the millennia, the Rhine and tributary rivers on each side filled the valley up. The relative youth of the terrain in the so-called lowlands, or the area near the lake, is evident from the reeds and the swamps most of which have only become dry over the course of the last century. Until a few centuries ago, peat was cut here and used as a heating fuel. Traces of the glacier are evident as 'glacier erosion', particularly on the rock faces along the Rhine valley.

All of which are things to ponder when walking or cycling along the shorelines of the lake, which is incidentally open to all visitors. That said, simply enjoying the natural surroundings, sailing and fishing boats on the lake is also more than enough. It is possible to explore the lake in all directions on a boat tour of Lake Constance, with the boat companies collaborating to offer a selection of routes. On such a tour, it is possible to gain a better impression of cycling or hiking options along the banks.

Ornithologists also enthuse about the bird life in the Rhine delta which originates from the year 1900. It was then that the new Rhine was partly re-channelled and also excavated in order to direct the water from the often torrential river on a straight trajectory into the lake to prevent the flooding of the valley which had previously often occurred during stormy weather. Work is still being completed to defuse the threat of the Rhine. The current goal is to provide it with more space to ensure the dam crest isn't breached in the event of flood waters.

This is an example of second hand nature, as near the market town of Hard, which was recently threatened with losing its name 'on Lake Constance' when its 50 m deep bay was completely flooded by the waters of new Rhine for the first time in 50 years. The bay was excavated and protected with a dam, and along the mouth of the Rhine which is now located further into the lake, biotopes have developed, maintained by specialist river workers and conservationists. This also applies in front of the Rhine delta, where the Polder dam forms a striking closure.

Die grandiose Vielfalt der Vorarlberger Landschaft ist auch Lebensraum für zahlreiche Tiere. Wer das Land aufmerksam durchstreift, erfreut sich vom Bodensee bis zum Hochgebirge an zahlreichen Begegnungen. Da lässt sich das wachsame Murmeltier beobachten, der in Österreich rare Rote Milan ist auf Beuteflug. Bei den Schleienlöchern am Bodenseeufer in Hard brütet der Haubentaucher und scheues Rehwild ist eigentlich in sämtlichen Landesteilen anzutreffen.

The impressively diverse Vorarlberg landscape is also home to many wild animals. Anyone who explores this region with their eyes open can count on numerous encounters, from Lake Constance to the highest peaks. The wary marmot is often to be seen. The red Milan, or red kite, is on the search for prey. The great crested grebe breeds on the banks of Lake Constance in Hard, and the timid roe deer can be seen all over the region.

Bregenz, die Landeshauptstadt, lässt sich nur wenig Raum zwischen dem Hausberg Pfänder und dem Bodensee. Hier saßen einst die Kelten, die Römer und Alemannen wohl auch deshalb, weil die schmale Klause gut zu verteidigen war. Im Dreißigjährigen Krieg umging das Schwedenheer unter General Wrangel diese stark befestigte Sperre und nahm Anfang 1647 die Stadt ein. Vom Besuch der Gäste aus dem Norden zeugen noch die Ruinen der alten Festung auf dem Gebhardsberg hoch über Bregenz, inzwischen von schwedischen Gästen wieder ebenso gern besucht wie von anderen. Und vom Pfänder schweift der Blick an Tagen mit klarem Wetter bis zum Turm des Münsters in Konstanz am anderen Ende des Sees. Der Rundblick umfasst das Allgäu und das Schweizer Rheintal bis weit zum Säntis und Churfirsten, auch die Dörfer, Täler und Erhebungen im Vorderen Bregenzerwald – ein idealer Ausguck, der den Begriff „überschaubar" für Österreichs kleinstes Bundesland verständlich macht. Auch im Hochsommer blitzt da manches Schneefeld von fernen Gipfeln.

Dazwischen liegt das Rheintal, in dem die Gemeinden und Städte langsam aufeinander zu wachsen. Der Druck ist groß und die Grünflächen bedürfen der Verteidigung. Ein optimal ausgebautes Netz an Rad- und Wanderwegen erschließt die unterschiedlichen Dorfkerne und verbindet die Städte, ebenso natürlich die Rheintalautobahn, die Eisenbahntrasse sowie ein besonders dichtes Netz an Busverbindungen. Alle Methoden der Fortbewegung erschließen den Blick auf eine gepflegte Gartenlandschaft mit Hausgärten und Streuobstanlagen.

Liegt im Herbst dichter Nebel über dem Rheintal, so wissen Sonnenhungrige ihre Plätze zu finden in den Hanggemeinden oder in kleinen Bergparzellen der Städte. In der Talmitte ragt der Kummenberg auf, der dem hartnäckigen Schleifen der Gletscher einst widerstand und dann als Lebensraum von Mensch und Tier gedient hatte. Weiter Richtung Oberland engt das Rheintal ein, vor der schmalsten Stelle, der Felsenau, liegt die Stadt Feldkirch. Nach der Klamm weitet sich der Walgau, durchflossen von der Ill. Auf markanten Erhebungen am Talrand zeugen etliche Burgruinen davon, dass das Gebiet im Mittelalter heftig umkämpft war. Im Appenzellerkrieg 1405 belagerten und erstürmten die erzürnten Schweizer eine Reihe von Burgen im Walgau. Am 20. April 1499 schließlich gewannen die Eidgenossen bei Frastanz eine wichtige Entscheidungsschlacht gegen den Schwäbischen Bund und die Habsburger Streitmacht. Im 18. und 19. Jahrhundert ging es dann friedlicher zu, als im Ortsteil Fellengatter Tabak angepflanzt und weit über Vorarlberg hinaus vertrieben wurde.
Auch in diesem Landesteil: Überschaubare Vielfalt, vom Talboden mit Feuchtwiesen bis empor zu den mächtigen steinernen Wächtern. Lang vor unserer Zeitrechnung hat der Mensch auch diese Gegend als Lebensraum zu schätzen gewusst, Ausgrabungen und Funde zeugen von Siedlungstätigkeit sowohl in der Steinzeit als auch in der Bronzezeit.

Es tut sich an Vorarlberger Gebirgshängen aber auch Wundersames. Auf der Rona Alpe, Gemeinde Bürserberg im Brandnertal, liegen auf über 1.200 Höhenmetern seit urdenklichen Zeiten haufenweise Felsbrocken, wie auch

Bregenz, the regional capital, nestles in comparatively little space between the Pfänder mountain and Lake Constance. This town has also been the seat of the Celts, the Romans and the Alemanni, all of whom found the compact hermitage easy to defend. During the thirty years war, the Swedish army led by General Wrangel breached the town's defences, capturing it in the year 1647. The ruins of the old fortifications on the Gebhardsberg high over Bregenz still pay testament to the visitors from the north, now often visited by Swedish tourists and those of other nationalities. And from the Pfänder, on clear days, the view stretches all the way to the tower of the cathedral in Konstanz. The panorama takes in the Allgäu and Swiss Rhine valley all the way to Säntis and Churfirsten, including the villages, valleys and hills towards the beginnings of the Bregenz Forest - one of the clear views for which Austria's smallest federal region is famed. And even at the peak of summer, snow can be seen to sparkle on the summits of the faraway peaks.

In between is the Rhine valley, with its gradually expanding communes and towns. The pressure on the undeveloped areas is considerable, and many green areas require defending. A superb network of cycling tracks and footpaths connects the villages and towns, in addition to the Rhine valley motorway, railway lines and a comprehensive network of bus routes. All modes of transport allow views of a well maintained market gardening landscape, with house gardens and mixed orchard developments.

If the Rhine valley is shrouded in a thick fog in the autumn, then those yearning for the sun head to the mountain villages or the higher areas of the towns. In the centre of the valley is the Kummenberg hill, which withstood the intense grinding of the glacier to later serve as living space for man and animal alike. The Rhine valley narrows towards Oberland, with the town of Feldkirch being situated before its narrowest point. After the gorge, the Walgau widens again, flowed through by the river Ill. The many castle ruins on the striking elevations along the edge of the valley pay witness to how the area was fought over in the Middle Ages. In the Appenzeller war of 1405, the incensed Swiss forces sieged and stormed many castles in Walgau. On 20th April 1499, the Swiss won a decisive battle at Frastanz against the Swabian League and the Habsburg army. In the 18th and 19th centuries life here was more peaceful. Tobacco was grown in the district of Fellengatter and sold far beyond Vorarlberg.
And also in this part of the region: a clear variety, from the valley floor with its wet meadows to the mighty stone guards towering above. Man also learned to value this area as a place of habitation long before our era, as shown by the archaeological digs and findings which prove that settlements existed here in both the Stone and Bronze Ages.

Strange things have also happened on the mountain slopes of the Vorarlberg. At 1,200 meters above sea level on the Rona alpine pasture in the district of Bürserberg in the Brandner valley, the kind of boulders are to be found which are also elsewhere in the valley. In 2004, a water diviner and commuter declared that these piles of rock, created by the glacier retreat and mountain formation to be stone circles. After this things progress quickly: a digger comes

Sie wirkt wie ein Relikt aus alter Zeit und eigentlich ist sie das auch, die „Mili", die alte Militärbadeanstalt vor dem Bregenzer Seeufer, bereits anno 1825 errichtet, um den Soldaten der nahen Kaserne das Schwimmen beizubringen. Ebenso wurden damals noch „Schwimmmanöver" mit bis zu 300 Soldaten durchgeführt. Inzwischen ist die Mili zivil und all den Stammgästen Erholungsort, die den Trubel eines großen Strandbades meiden. Und wo sonst bietet sich schon die Möglichkeit, direkt vom Liegeplatz per „Köpfler", also per Kopfsprung in den See zu gelangen?

It looks like a relic from a bygone era which is actually what it is - the 'Mili' - the old military bathing institute in front of the Bregenz lakeside. It was built in 1825 to introduce the soldiers of the nearby barracks to swimming. In those days, 'swimming manoeuvres' with up to 300 soldiers were carried out. The 'Mili' is now open to the public and a place of relaxation and recreation to its many regular guests, who are spared the stress of an open swimming area. And where else offers visitors the opportunity to dive straight into the lake from their chosen spot head-first?

sonst im ganzen Tal. Anno 2004 ernennt ein Rutengänger und Pendler diese durch Gebirgsbildung und Gletscherrückzug entstandenen Gesteinshaufen zu Steinkreisen. Daraufhin geht es rasch: Hier ein paar Felstrümmer per Bagger weggeräumt, dort einige umherliegende Brocken um mehrere Meter verrückt und senkrecht gestellt – schon sind die Steinkreise fertig. Was stört es, dass archäologische Grabungen durch Fachleute keinen einzigen Hinweis auf menschliches Einwirken erbringen? Die Steinkreise stehen jetzt auf der Rona Alpe und bis in 1.000 Jahren sind sie ganz gewiss historisch ...
Die Rona Alpe ist natürlich ebenso wie zahlreiche andere dennoch lohnendes Ziel für Wanderer, die Majestät der Gipfel mag wohl erheblich mehr zu beeindrucken als eingebildete Steinzeit-Wegweiser oder Kultplätze.

Landschaft. In Vorarlberg gehört bei diesem Thema ganz gewiss auch der Bregenzerwald eigens angeführt. Da thronen eindrucksvolle Höfe auf Voralpenhügeln, freundliche, überschaubare Dörfer sind aufgereiht. Hier sind Naturgenuss und eine besondere Verwöhnkultur miteinander im Einklang und die Freizeitangebote beziehen mit ein, was die Landschaft großzügig darbietet. Vorarlberg, das Land der kurzen Wege – auch in dieser Talschaft ist es meist ein Katzensprung vom sanften Hang zum schroffen Fels, und wer die Thermik zu nutzen versteht und den Gleitschirm zu bedienen, dem gelingt ein Sprung auch auf größere Entfernung.

Die Vorarlberger sind stolz auf die Landschaft, in der sie leben dürfen und die sie gern mit Gästen teilen. Im Einvernehmen mit den Nachbarn in Tirol, im Fürstentum Liechtenstein, der Schweiz und Deutschland hüten sie ein Kleinod mit vielen Facetten. Es lassen sich täglich neue davon entdecken.

in and tidies away some of the stray rocks, some of the rocks are then moved a few meters and placed upright - and the stone circle is finished. Of course, the fact that digs by professional archaeologists have found no evidence of human activity here is quietly brushed aside. The stone circles are now standing on the Rona pasture where they're set to be historic for at least another 1,000 years ...
Like numerous others, the Rona alpine pasture is a worthwhile destination for hikers and the majesty of the summits far more impressive than imaginary stone circles or places of worship.

Landscape. In Vorarlberg, the Bregenz Forest is certainly worthy a separate mention in this respect. Impressive farms sit enthroned on alpine pastures, friendly, approachable villages sit in rows. Here, the enjoyment of nature and a particular culture of pampering and recreation are in accord, with leisure facilities incorporating what the landscape generously offers. Vorarlberg, the region of the short distances - in this valley it is usually only a stone's throw from the soft slope to the craggy rock face, and those who know how to make use of thermal currents and operate a paraglider are able to complete such 'throws' over even longer distances.

The local people of the Vorarlberg are proud of the landscape in which they are privileged to live and which they are glad to share with visitors. In amicable agreement with their neighbours in Tyrol, in the principality of Liechtenstein, in Switzerland and in Germany, they jealously guard a jewel with many facets - more of which can be discovered every day.

Jedes Jahr wechselt diese Segelregatta auf dem Bodensee die Richtung: 2008 heißt sie deshalb „Ost-West-Regatta", 2009 eben „West-Ost". Der Bregenzer Segel-Club und der Konstanzer Yacht Club laden ein und 2008 segeln über 200 Boote mit. Am frühen Morgen gehört der See ganz den Seebären, die hier vor der Bucht von Bregenz und Hard versuchen, den vorhandenen Wind optimal zu nützen, um Richtung Konstanz zu gelangen. Ganz rechts im Bild noch die vorgestreckte Mündung des Alpenrheins in den See.
Gegen die Sonne wirkt die gekräuselte Oberfläche des Wassers wie gehämmertes Silber (kleines Bild).

This sailing regatta on Lake Constance changes its direction every year: In 2008 it is therefore to be called the 'East-West' Regatta, and in 2009, the 'West-East'. The Bregenz Sailing club and the Konstanz Yacht Club are taking part, and in 2008 more than 200 are to set sail. In the early morning, the lake, which is often shrouded in mist, belongs to the sea bears, who are here attempting to make optimum use of the wind, swimming from the bays of Bregenz and Hard to Konstanz. To the far right of the picture is the estuary of the Alpine Rhine and the lake. The rippled surface of the water looks like wrought silver against the sun (small image).

Erst 1989 hielt der Golfsport auch in Vorarlberg Einzug, im Montafon konnte damals der erste Golfplatz bespielt werden. Inzwischen stehen den Golfern im Land bereits sechs Plätze zur Verfügung, der jüngste 18-Loch-Platz wird vom Golfclub Montfort in Rankweil betrieben. Golflandschaft im Rankweiler Weitried aus der Vogelperspektive, mit Greens und Sandbunkern.

The sport of Golf arrived in the Vorarlberg in 1989 with the first course to open being in Montafon. Golfers are now able to take their pick of six courses, with the most recent 18 hole course to open being in Rankweil, run by Montfort Golf Club. A bird's eye view of the golf landscape at Weitried, Rankweil, with the greens and bunkers.

Nein, die beiden Hohenemser Bergsteiger Konrad Mathis und Mark Amann sind weder auf einem Salzsee unterwegs noch in einer Mondlandschaft. Sie queren die Sporaplatte, die gewaltige Felsenplatte am Fuß der Drei Türme am Abschluss des Gauertales. Die von der Kraft des Wassers signierte Sporaplatte endet an den senkrecht aufragenden Felswänden des großen und mittleren der Drei Türme, der kleine Turm links ist durch das Sporatobel abgeteilt. Auf seiner Spitze verläuft die Grenze zwischen Vorarlberg und dem Schweizer Kanton Graubünden.

No, Hohenems climbers Konrad Mathis and Mark Amann are neither crossing a salt lake nor in a lunar landscape. They're crossing the 'Sporaplatte' the massive rock plate at the foot of the 'three towers' at the end of the Gauertal valley. The Sporaplatte, autographed by the power of water, ends at the vertical rock face of the large and medium of the three towers. The small tower on the left is partitioned by the Sporatobel. The border between Vorarlberg and the Swiss canton of Graubünden traverses its summit.

Vogelfreunde sind erfreut, die 16 Vorarlberger Berufsfischer auf dem Bodensee entsetzt: Die Population der Kormorane hat deutlich zugenommen, wie diese Aufnahme vom Rheinholz zeigt, der Mündung des Alten Rheins bei Gaißau. Auf der Pfahlward, die ein weiteres Wegschwemmen des gefährdeten Ufers verhindern soll, sitzen die gefräßigen Vögel, die täglich auf Beutezug gehen und dabei 500 bis 700 g Fisch verdrücken.

In den Bregenzer Seenanlagen streiten sich im futterarmen Winter zahllose Möwen um wenige Brotbrocken. Etliche Tauben bleiben in diesem Gewirr lieber ruhig auf ihrer Stange sitzen und hoffen auf einige übrig gebliebene Brosamen.

Bird lovers may be pleased, but the 16 professional Vorarlberg fishermen certainly aren't: the local population of cormorants has recently undergone a big increase, as is plain to see on this image of Rheinholz at the mouth of the river Rhine, Gaißau. The gluttonous birds sit on the pile wall which is intended to prevent a further washing away of the endangered river bank. Each bird, often circling for prey, eats from 500 to 700 g of fish every day. In lean winter times, a flock of seagulls squabbles over some scraps of bread at the Bregenz lakeside. Many choose to remain on their perch, in the hope of retrieving a few of the remaining breadcrumbs.

Die Jahreszeiten als begnadete Landschaftsgestalter. Eiskalter Herbstnebel überzieht Bäume und Schilfrohr am Rohrspitz mit Raureif, nach dem Ende der kalten Jahreszeit peitscht dort Frühjahrswind Bäume und junge Schilfpflanzen.

The seasons – as landscape architects in their own right. An ice cold autumn fog enshrouds the trees and glazed frosted reeds at Rohrspitz. When the cold time of the year is over, spring winds whip these trees and young reed plants.

Wasser und Gestein. Das Feiatobel (oben) ist ein verstecktes Naturjuwel zwischen Dornbirn und Hohenems. Nähere Angaben zur Lage des plätschernden Kleinods sind dem Fotografen nicht zu entlocken ... Anders ist das bei der Breitachklamm im Kleinwalsertal (rechts), die ganz offiziell durchwandert werden kann.

Water and stone. The Feiatobel (above) is a hidden jewel of nature between Dornbirn and Hohenems. The photographer was unable to find out further information about the position of the rippling treasure ... Things are different at the Breitachklamm gorge in the Little Walser Valley (right) through which visitors are officially able to wander.

Das Spiel von Licht und Schatten verzaubert die Umgebung dieser Hütte oberhalb von Nesslegg am Hochtannberg. Die Schafherde zeigt sich davon aber keineswegs beeindruckt.

The interplay of light and shade enchants these huts and their surroundings above Nesslegg on the Hochtannberg pass. The herd of sheep is oblivious to such trivial matters, however.

Im Körbersee unweit von Schröcken am Hochtannberg spiegeln sich markante Erhebungen des Lechquellengebirges, links der Hochberg, rechts die Künzelspitze.

Prominent peaks of the Lechquellengebirge mountain range are reflected in the Körbersee near Schröcken on the Hochtannberg pass. On the left the Hochberg, on the right, the Künzelspitze.

Wandern, genießen, horchen, staunen – der Tafamunter Augstenberg ist ein Beispiel dafür, dass neben geübten Kletterern auch Wanderer das Verwallgebiet erkunden können. Im Winter ziehen Tourengeher von hier ihre Spuren durch Tiefschneehänge.

Walk, enjoy, listen and marvel – the Tafamunter Augstenberg is an example of how with seasoned climbers, ramblers are also able to enjoy the Verwall area. In the winter here, ski hikers leave their tracks behind in deep snow.

Die Bergwelt Vorarlbergs präsentiert dem Wanderer einen reichen Blumengarten. Bilder oben: die Sünserspitze nahe dem Furkapass, einmal mit Arnika, dann mit Alpenrosen als Schmuck. Im Frühjahr ziert sich das Zugertal mit der Roten Wand im Hintergrund mit Himmelschlüsseln, rechts das Omeshorn in Oberlech mit einer Zierde aus Butterblumen.

Ramblers and hikers can take their pick from an impressive selection of flowers in the Vorarlberg region. Pictures above: the Sünserspitze near the Furka pass, once adorned with leopard's bane, once with alpine roses. In the spring, the Zugertal valley, overlooked by the Rote Wand mountain, is covered in cowslip, and to the right, the Omeshorn in Oberlech, carpeted with buttercups.

Auf der rechten Seite eine Magerwiese in reicher Vielfalt an Blumen, Gräsern und Kräutern, wie sie dem Alpvieh in Vorarlberg sommers als Futter dient. Im Hintergrund die kleine Künzelspitze bei Nesslegg, Hochtannberg.

On the right page: a rough pasture with a rich variety of flowers, grass and herbs, which will be fodder to the alpine livestock in the Vorarlberg summer. In the background: the lower Künzelspitze near Nesslegg, Hochtannberg.

Vielfalt einer Landschaft. Links der Blick über das Vergaldener Tal in Gargellen mit Blick auf die Silvretta. Der Sporn in der Bildmitte ist der Litzner, rechts daneben das Große Seehorn.

The diversity of a landscape. Left: the aspect over the Vergalden valley in Gargellen with a view of the Silvretta. The peak in the centre of the image is the Litzner, to the right of the 'Grosse Seehorn'.

Auf der rechten Seite die akkurate Pyramide des Plansott im Walserkamm, der den Walgau vom Laternsertal trennt, gesehen vom Gehrenfalben.

Right page: the accurate pyramid of the Plansott in Walserkamm, which separates the Walgau from the Laternser valley, viewed from Gehrenfalben.

Atemberaubender Ausblick von der Höferspitze im Kleinwalsertal Richtung Biberkopf an der Grenze von Vorarlberg, Tirol und Bayern.

The breathtaking view from the peak of the Höferspitze in the Little Walser Valley looking towards Biberkopf on the border between Vorarlberg, the Tyrol and Bavaria.

Ein hochalpines Gewässer ist der Lünersee, 1959 wurde seine Speicherkapazität durch eine Staumauer erheblich vergrößert. Die Vorarlberger Illwerke nützen das Wasser aus dem am Abschluss des Brandnertales gelegenen See für die Stromerzeugung im Lünerseewerk. Die Douglasshütte, auf 1.979 m Höhe direkt am See gelegen, bietet Wanderern und Bergsteigern insgesamt 150 Schlafplätze.

The Lünersee: a high alpine lake. In 1959 its capacity was substantially increased through a dam. The Vorarlberg Illwerke use the water from this lake, which is situated at the end of the Brander valley, to generate electricity at the Lünersee power station. The Douglasshütte hotel, situated right on the lake at 1,979 m, offers 150 beds to ramblers and climbers alike.

Sie ziehen sich wegen der Erwärmung unseres Klimas immer rascher zurück, die Eispanzer um die höchsten Gipfel, noch aber beeindrucken sie wie rechts der Ochsentaler Gletscher in der Silvretta und oben der Brandner Ferner unterhalb der Schesaplana.

Although they may be retreating at an ever faster rate due to global warming, the ice crusts on the highest peaks remain an impressive sight as you can see on the right, the Ochstental glacier in the Silvretta, and above, the Brandner Ferner below the Schesaplana.

SEITE 140 /141
Heftiger Wind verwirbelt den ersten Schnee, der auf der Alpe „Alter Hof" unterhalb des Alpkopfes in Dornbirn gefallen ist. Am Hang unterhalb des Felsabbruchs markiert der Schnee den steilen Weg, den das Vieh nimmt, wenn es über das Fluhlöchle von der Alpe Unterfluh zur Alpe Bindel zieht.

Heavy winds buffet the first snows to have fallen on the 'Alter Hof' alpine pasture beneath the Alpkopf in Dornbirn. On the hillside beneath the rock fall, the snow marks the steep paths taken by the livestock as it wends its way over the Fluhlöchle pass from the Unterfluh to Bindel alpine pastures.

Winter im Verwall, gesehen von der Mondspitze aus. Links die Omesspitze nahe dem Skigebiet am Sonnenkopf, in der Bildmitte die Eisentälispitzen.

Winter in Verwall, as viewed from the Mondspitze. To the left, the Omesspitze near the Sonnenkopf skiing area, and in the centre of the photograph, the Eisentälispitzen.

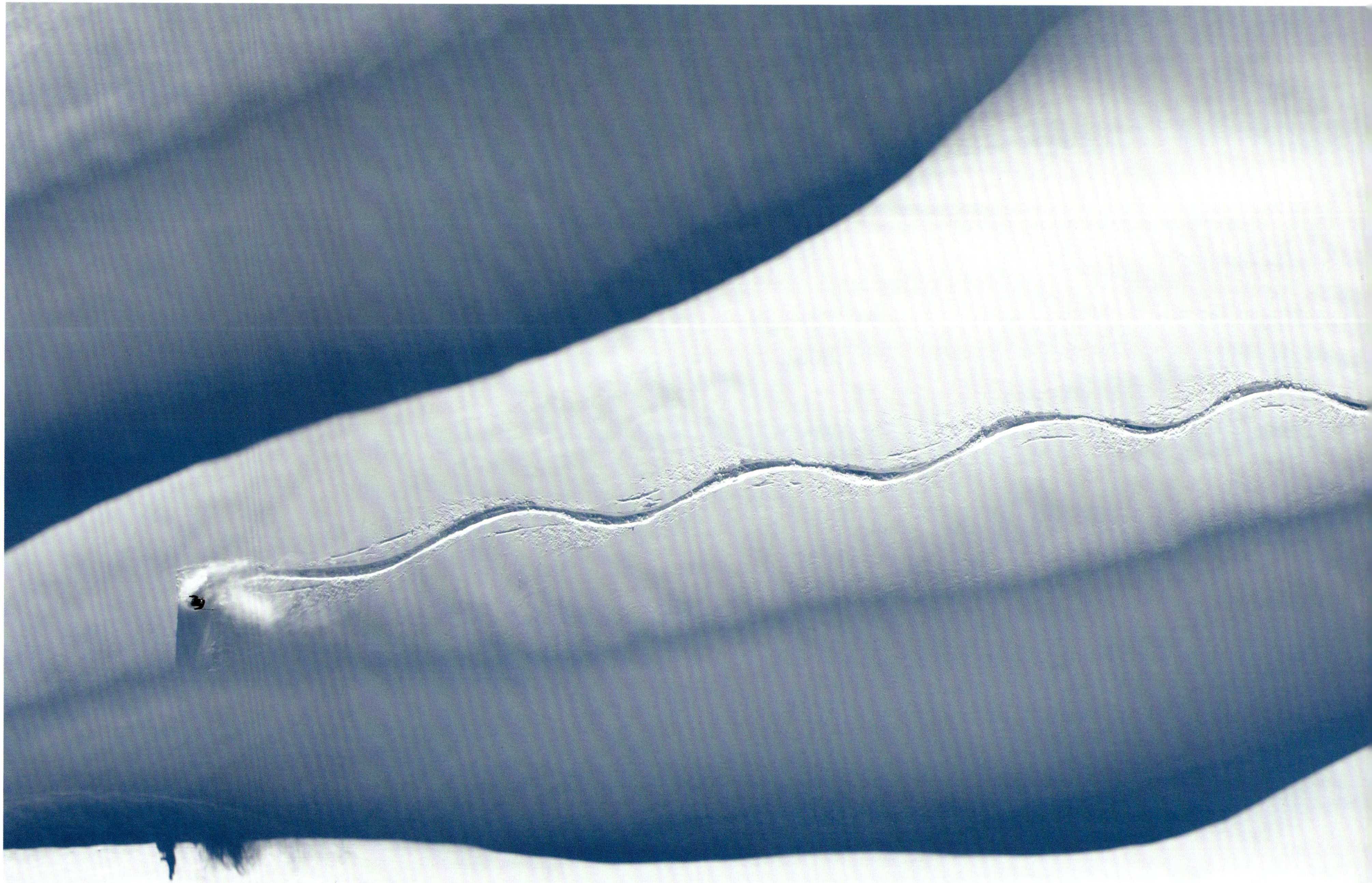

SEITE 144 / 145

Spuren im Schnee. Das Schneetäli bei Lech (links) verdient seinen Namen ganz gewiss. Rechts; Tourengeher beim Aufstieg zum Falzkopf unweit des Diedamskopfes bei Schoppernau im Bregenzerwald.

Tracks in the snow. The Schneetäli (snowy valley) is certainly worthy of its name. Right: ski hikers making their ascent to the Falzkopf near the Diedamskopf at Schoppenau in the Bregenz Forest.

Dem Traum von Freiheit ein gewaltiges Stück näher kommen – in dieser Landschaft nützen immer mehr begeisterte Sportler diese Chance. Schneeabenteuer mit Freerider Florian Köfer in der Flexenmulde, mit Blick ins Klostertal, das sich noch im Nebel versteckt. Auf dem Bild rechts reicht der gleiche Blick noch etwas weiter, im Hintergrund ragt am Abschluss des Brandnertales die Schesaplana empor.

Mountain adventures to get nearer to the dream of freedom - an opportunity gladly taken in this area by more and more sports enthusiasts. Fun in the snow of the Flexenmulde with free-rider Florian Köfer, with views over a mist-shrouded Kloster valley. In the photograph on the right, the same view stretches somewhat further, with the Schesaplana towering proudly above the end of the Brandner valley.

Der Winter schafft Skulpturen aus Schneekristallen auf dem Maiensäß oberhalb der Rheintalgemeinde Fraxern, mit dem Täler übergreifenden Blick auf den Rätikon.

The winter creates snow-crystal sculptures at Maiensäß above the Rhine valley commune of Fraxern, with a valley-spanning view towards the Rätikon.

SEITE 150 / 151
Abendstimmung auf dem tief verschneiten Fraxner First. Von diesem Aussichtspunkt schweift der Blick bis zum Hochhäderich im Vorderen Bregenzerwald (Bildmitte).

The evening atmosphere on the very snowy Fraxner First. From this vantage point, the views stretch as far as the Hochhäderich at the outskirts of the Bregenz Forest (centre of the image).

Herzlichen Dank!

Bei allen, die zum Werden von „Leidenschaft Vorarlberg" beigetragen haben, möchten wir uns ganz herzlich bedanken!

Viele der im Buch vertretenen Personen haben einige Geduld aufgebracht, bis ich das Foto gemacht hatte, das ich mir vorgestellt habe. Andere haben mir Türen geöffnet und Zugänge ermöglicht, haben Informationen beigetragen und Kontakte vermittelt.

Der erfahrene Pilot Dr. Peter Mennel ermöglichte gekonnt Aufnahmen aus der Vogel- oder besser der Hubschrauber-Perspektive. Rudi Burtscher von der Getzner Textil AG, Armin Bernhart von der Firma Baur Prüf- und Messtechnik sowie Heimo Lubetz, Blum Beschläge, und Werner Amann, Illwerke AG, zeigten sich sehr hilfsbereit. Ebenso hilfreich waren die Familie Bechter vom Hotel „Schiffle", der Trachtenverein Sonntag im Großen Walsertal, die Bauernfamilien Rüf und Klocker sowie Priorin Maria Cordis Feuerstein vom Kloster Marienberg, Bregenz.

„Leidenschaft Vorarlberg" ist dank dieser Unterstützung zu einem runden Werk geworden, das einen Eindruck zu vermitteln vermag von der Vielfalt der besiedelten Landschaft zwischen Arlberg und Bodensee.

Wir freuen uns, dieses Werk präsentieren zu dürfen.

Peter Mathis und Alfons J. Kopf

Thank You!

We would like to offer our most sincere thanks to everyone who contributed to the coming into being of 'A Passion for Vorarlberg'!

I demanded a considerable amount of patience from many of the people featured in this book until I was able to get the photo of them that I wanted. Other people opened doors to me, provided me with access, contributed information, or provided me with valuable contacts.

The experienced Pilot, Dr. Peter Mennel, made expert photographs possible from the bird's eye view or even better, the helicopter perspective. Rudi Burtscher from the company Getzner Textil AG, Armin Bernhart from the company 'Baur Prüf- und Messtechnik', Heimo Lubetz of 'Blum Beschläge', and Werner Amann of 'Illwerke AG', were all extremely helpful. The Bechter family from the Schiffle Hotel, the 'Trachtenverein Sonntag' in the Great Walser Valley, the farming families Rüf and Klocker, as well as Prioress Maria Cordis Feuerstein of Marienberg Convent, Bregenz, were also very helpful.

It is thanks to this support that 'A Passion for Vorarlberg' became a rounded work capable of providing an impression of the diversity of the colonised landscape between Arlberg and Lake Constance.

We feel pleased to be able to present this work.

Peter Mathis and Alfons J. Kopf